Nelson Advanced Modular Science

Physical and Inorganic Chemistry: Applications

ALAN JARVIS • ROD BEAVON

Nelson

Thomas Nelson UK

Nelson House
Mayfield Road
Walton-on-Thames
Surrey KT12 5PL
United Kingdom

I(T)P® Thomas Nelson is an International Thomson Company
I(T)P® is used under licence

ISBN 0 17 448258 2
9 8 7 6 5 4 3 2 1
01 00 99 98

Picture research by Image Select International
Paging and illusration by Hardlines, Charlbury, Oxfordshire
Printed in Italy by Eurografica S.p.A, Vicenza

Acknowledgements
The author and publishers are grateful to the following for permission to reproduce copyright images:

Alcan: 6.8
British Steel/PPL: 2.9, 6.9
Chris Fairclough 7.7
Elida Faberge: 5.5
Image Select: 2.2, 2.10
Peter Gould 4.3f
Philip Harris Ltd. 2.6
Science Photo Library: 1.1; 1.2; 2.7 (John Mead); 4.3a, 4.3d, 7.2 (Andrew McClenaghan); 4.3b, 4.3c, 4.3e, 7.3 (Jerry Mason); 4.4 a-c (Imperial College); 5.4 (Martin Bond); 5.6a and b (Tommaso Guicciardini); 5.7 (NASA); 7.1 (Claude Nuridsany and Marie Perennou); 7.5a (Chemical Design Ltd) 7.5b (Dr Jeremy Burgess).
Tony Stone Images: 6.8 (George Haling)

Contents

Introduction

This textbook is one of a series of four produced in response to demand from students and their teachers for resource material supporting the modular chemistry courses which lead to examinations set by Edexcel London Examinations. There has been a widespread development of modular courses at Advanced level, and Edexcel embarked on a modular format in September 1994. There is also an ever-present pressure on syllabus writers to introduce new material into syllabuses to ensure that they reflect adequately the role of chemistry in society today, whilst retaining the principal core concepts laid down by common agreement and by the Qualifications and Curriculum Authority. The writers of the new syllabuses and of these texts have endeavoured to balance these conflicting demands.

There is a bewildering variety of chemistry texts discussing aspects of the subject at an appropriate level for the A-level student, and it is not the intention of this series to divert the attention of students from these. Indeed, it is hoped that students will be excited by their study of chemistry and will want to pursue specialist avenues of interest, as countless others have done in years past. However, it is recognised that at certain times students seek a text which will encapsulate in a relatively small volume the outline of necessary study for each of the Edexcel modules in chemistry.

These volumes are writen by the examiners, all experienced teachers, specifically to prepare students for these examinations and all the necessary basic material of the syllabus is covered. They further prompt and give pointers for further study for the interested student.

We hope that students will find these texts helpful and supportive of their studies at A-level and their preparation for examinations, and also stimulating to further reading in a wider context.

Geoff Barraclough
Chemistry Series Editor

The authors

Alan Jarvis was head of Chemistry at Stoke-on-Trent Sixth Form College and was a chief examiner in Chemistry for Edexcel London Examinations. He died in July 1997.

Rod Beavon is a Chief Examiner in Chemistry for Edexcel London Examinationsand Head of Science at Westminster School, London.

Ionic crystals

Why does sodium react with chlorine to give sodium chloride? The simple 'explanation' says that in doing so both sodium and chlorine achieve, in their ions, a noble gas electron structure. This is of course true; but it is only part of the story. The production of the ions is overall endothermic — and it is the bringing together of these separate ions into the solid crystal that is exothermic enough to compensate.

Lattice enthalpy

Some of the enthalpy changes have been met before in Module 1 (see *Structure, Bonding and the Periodic Table*): the first ionisation energy for sodium, which is the energy change per mole for

$$Na(g) \rightarrow Na^+(g) + e^-$$

and the electron affinity of chlorine, which is the energy change per mole for the process

$$Cl(g) + e^- \rightarrow Cl^-(g),$$

are significant here, together with the enthalpy of formation of sodium chloride, defined as the enthalpy change per mole for

$$Na(s) + \tfrac{1}{2}Cl_2(g) \rightarrow NaCl(s)$$

These can be combined using Hess's Law, together with the enthalpies of atomisation of the elements, when the significance of the lattice enthalpy, ΔH_{latt}, becomes evident. First we shall remind ourselves about Hess's Law and define lattice enthalpy.

Hess's Law revisited

In Module 2 (see *Principles of Physical and Organic Chemistry*) Hess's Law was introduced. The heat energy change (enthalpy change) for a reaction depends only on the initial and final states of the system, and not on the pathway between those states. It was used there to calculate enthalpy changes for reactions which cannot be found by experiment, by combining the enthalpy changes of other, possible, reactions. The use of enthalpies of formation and of combustion in this way will be familiar.

The first ionisation energy is the amount of energy required to remove a mole of electrons from a mole of atoms in the gas phase to form a mole of singly positive ions, that is

$$M(g) = M^+(g) + e^-$$

Use standard enthalpies of combustion to find the enthalpy change for the reaction

$$CH_3CH_2COOH(l) + H_2(g) \rightarrow CH_3CH_2CHO(l) + H_2O(l)$$

$\Delta H_c^{\circ}/kJ\ mol^{-1}$: $CH_3CH_2COOH(l)$ –1527; $H_2(g)$ –286; $CH_3CH_2CHO(l)$ –1821.

Use standard enthalpies of formation to find the enthalpy changes for the reactions:

(a) $CH_3OH(l) + CH_3COOH(l) \rightarrow CH_3COOCH_3(l) + H_2O(l)$

(b) $CH_3OH(l) + HCl(g) \rightarrow CH_3Cl(g) + H_2O(l)$

(c) $CH_3I(l) + H_2O(g) \rightarrow CH_3OH(l) + HI(g)$

$\Delta H_f^{\circ}/kJ\ mol^{-1}$: $CH_3OH(l)$ –239; $CH_3COOH(l)$ –485; $CH_3COOCH_3(l)$ –446; $H_2O(l)$ –286;

$HCl(g)$ –92; $CH_3Cl(g)$ –82; $CH_3I(l)$ –16; $HI(g)$ +27

The First Law of Thermodynamics
Energy cannot be created or destroyed. It can only be converted from one form to another.

IONIC CRYSTALS

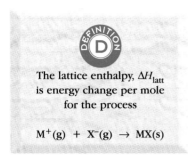

The lattice enthalpy, ΔH_{latt} is energy change per mole for the process

$$M^+(g) + X^-(g) \rightarrow MX(s)$$

Figure 1.1   Fritz Haber

Figure 1.2   Max Born

The lattice enthalpy

The lattice enthalpy (lattice energy) of sodium chloride is defined as the energy change per mole for the process

$$Na^+(g) + Cl^-(g) \rightarrow NaCl(s)$$

In general it is the energy change for the formation of one mole of the solid crystal from the gaseous ions. This definition means that lattice enthalpies are exothermic; many books define this quantity in the endothermic direction, so make sure you know which convention is being used.

Lattice enthalpies are large. It is this large energy release that enables the reaction of sodium and chlorine to take place, and this is shown in the Born–Haber cycle (see Figure 1.1).

Enthalpy changes

The enthalpy changes involved in the Born–Haber cycle can be defined more formally (and generally):

• $\Delta H_a^\ominus$, the standard enthalpy of atomisation, is the heat energy change for the production of one mole of atoms in the gas phase from the element in its standard state. Note that it is defined per mole of atoms formed;

• $I(1)$, the first ionisation energy, is the energy change for the conversion of one mole of gaseous atoms into one mole of positive ions in the gas phase;

$$M(g) \rightarrow M^+(g) + e^-$$

• The second ionisation energy is defined similarly, being the energy change per mole for the process

$$M^+(g) \rightarrow M^{2+}(g) + e^-$$

• E.A.(1) is the first electron affinity, which is the energy change for the conversion of one mole of gaseous atoms into one mole of negative ions in the gas phase;

$$X(g) + e^- \rightarrow X^-(g).$$

• The second electron affinity is defined similarly:

$$X^-(g) + e^- \rightarrow X^{2-}(g)$$

• $\Delta H_f^\ominus$, the standard enthalpy of formation, is the heat energy change accompanying the formation of one mole of compound from its elements, all substances being in their standard states at 1 atm pressure and defined temperature.

All of the above can be obtained experimentally, either directly or, in some cases, indirectly via other Hess's Law cycles.

The lattice enthalpy cannot be experimentally determined; it can only be found by using the Born–Haber cycle. Nevertheless this value is called the experimental value of ΔH_{latt} since the Born–Haber cycle uses experimentally-determined values. The value thus obtained is the lattice enthalpy which the compound actually possesses; it is the real lattice enthalpy. The distinction between this and the theoretical or calculated lattice enthalpy is discussed on page 8.

Watch that sign: a source of errors

Many errors in thermochemical calculations can be laid at the door of the simple signs + and –. The problem is that they are used in several ways:

- as an instruction: a + b means 'add the number b to the number a'. This use of +, as an instruction, is called a binary operation since it is an operation on two things. Other binary operations include those represented by –, ×, and ÷.

- as an indication of whether a number is greater than zero (+12) or less than zero (–2).

- and, in chemistry, as a convention, to indicate the direction of movement of heat; + into the system, and – out of the system.

Errors can be reduced dramatically if you distinguish, in your calculations, between the instruction to add or subtract, and the sign convention; this is done in the examples below by using brackets to separate the instruction + (add) from the convention + (endothermic).

The Born–Haber cycle

The Born–Haber cycle relates all of the enthalpy changes mentioned earlier to the lattice enthalpy. It can be shown in two ways, one as an energy-level diagram, the other as a cycle, whichever seems more clear.

The energy-level diagram for the Born–Haber cycle for sodium chloride is given in figure 1.3. Each horizontal line represents the energy level, the species existing on this level being written on the line together with their states. The gaps represent the enthalpy changes accompanying the change in the species shown, and can be drawn to scale if desired.

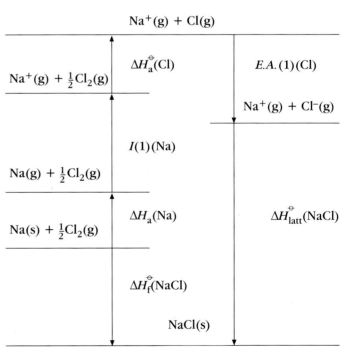

Figure 1.3 The energy-level form of the Born-Haber cycle for sodium chloride.

The cycle form for sodium chloride is shown in fig 1.2, below.

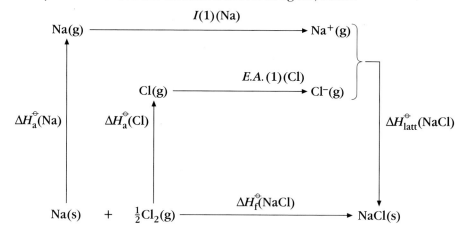

Figure 1.4 The cycle form of the Born-Haber Cycle for sodium chloride.

From both of these diagrams we have:

$$\Delta H_f^{\ominus}(\text{NaCl}) = \Delta H_a^{\ominus}(\text{Na}) + \Delta H_a^{\ominus}(\text{Cl}) + I(1)(\text{Na}) + \text{E.A.}(1)(\text{Cl}) + \Delta H_{latt}^{\ominus}(\text{NaCl}).$$

Substituting values in kJ mol^{-1}, and remembering to use brackets to distinguish signs, we obtain:

$$(-411) = (+109) + (+121) + (+494) + (-364) + \Delta H_{latt}(\text{NaCl})$$

from which

$$\Delta H_{latt}(\text{NaCl}) = -771 \text{ kJ mol}^{-1}$$

QUESTION

Draw a Born-Haber cycle for lithium fluoride, and use it to find the lattice enthalpy for LiF.

Data/kJ mol^{-1}:

First ionisation energy of lithium   +520

Enthalpy of atomisation of lithium   +159

Enthalpy of atomisation of fluorine   +79

Electron affinity of fluorine   – 328

Enthalpy of formation of LiF   – 616

Factors affecting the magnitude of the lattice enthalpy

The lattice enthalpy depends on the sizes of the ions, on their charges, on the crystal structure of the compound, and on the extent to which the bonding deviates from the fully ionic model.

The lattice of an ionic crystal is held together by a balance of attractive forces between ions of opposite charge and repulsive forces between those of like charge; overall there is net attraction.

The force between two charges q_1 and q_2 is given by Coulomb's Law (which you need not learn):

$$F = \frac{q_1 q_2}{kd^2}$$

where F is the magnitude of the force

      q_1 and q_2 are the charges

      d is the distance between the centres of the charges

      k is a constant which depends on what is between the charges.

      (In the case of an ionic crystal there is a vacuum).

From this it is clear that the lattice enthalpy will increase

• as the magnitudes of the charges q_1 and q_2 increase

• as the distance d between the ions decreases.

Lattice enthalpies are therefore larger for compounds of small group 2 cations with small anions, than for larger group 1 cations with large anions. Experimental values for the lattice enthalpies of the halides of group 1 and the chlorides and oxides of group 2 are given in Tables 1.1 and 1.2.

Table 1.1 *Experimental lattice enthalpies in kJ mol^{-1} for the alkali metal halides.*

	Fluoride	Chloride	Bromide	Iodide
lithium	−1031	−848	−803	−759
sodium	−918	−780	−742	−705
potassium	−817	−711	−679	−651
rubidium	−783	−685	−656	−628
caesium	−747	−661	−635	−613

Draw a Born-Haber cycle for calcium sulphide, and use it to find the lattice enthalpy for CaS. Suggest reasons for the difference between the value obtained and the lattice enthalpy of CaO , which is −3401 kJ mol^{-1}.
Data/kJ mol^{-1}:

First ionisation energy of calcium	+590
Second ionisation energy of calcium	+1145
First electron affinity of sulphur	−200
Second electron affinity of sulphur	+640
Enthalpy of atomisation of sulphur	+278
Enthalpy of atomisation of calcium	+178
Enthalpy of formation of CaS	−482

The alkali metal halides show the effect of increasing size of action or anion; ΔH_{latt} decreases in magnitude from LiF to CsF, or from LiF to LiI, since in both cases the distance between the ions is increasing. The strongest lattice is LiF, with the smallest ions; the weakest is CsI, with the largest. A word of caution, however; our comparisons are less quantitative than they might appear. The comparisons would require that all the crystal structures considered are the same, but they are not. The lattice enthalpy depends on the crystal structure as well as on the ions, since the distance between the ions depends on the structure that is adopted.

ΔH_{latt} would be expected to be larger for group 2 halides, since the cation is more highly charged and smaller than group 1, and even larger for oxides, where both ions have a double charge and the radius of the oxide ion (140 pm) is less than that of the chloride ion (180 pm). Table 1.2 shows that both these predictions are true.

Table 1.2 *Experimental lattice enthalpies in kJ mol^{-1} for Group 2 chlorides and oxides.*

$MgCl_2$	−2493	MgO	−3889
$CaCl_2$	−2237	CaO	−3513
$SrCl_2$	−2112	SrO	−3310
$BaCl_2$	−2018	BaO	−3152

ΔH_{latt} and experiment

It was stated above that ΔH_{latt} cannot be determined experimentally. It is reasonable to ask why not; surely if NaCl were heated sufficiently, gas phase ions would be produced? Alas, it is not so; sodium chloride vapour at temperatures not much above its boiling temperature of 1413°C consists of ion pairs Na$^+$Cl$^-$. Raising the temperature causes dissociation into atoms Na and Cl, and not into ions. Indeed the high lattice enthalpy of sodium chloride would lead to a much higher boiling temperature than it actually has if these ion pairs were not formed. On boiling not all the interionic forces found in the solid state are broken.

Applying the lattice enthalpy

Lattice enthalpies are useful in considering a variety of problems:

- the stoichiometry of salts, for example why magnesium chloride is $MgCl_2$ and not MgCl;

- the solubility of ionic compounds;

- the thermal decomposition of salts.

Each of these will now be considered.

The stoichiometry of salts

The word stoichiometry, referring to the ratios in which atoms combine or react, comes from Greek, meaning element measurer. Students often ask: why isn't the formula for magnesium chloride MgCl rather than $MgCl_2$?

The answer can be found from the Born–Haber cycle. All chemical bonding occurs because the system of bound atoms (a molecule, or an ionic or metallic lattice) is of lower energy than the separated atoms. The Born–Haber cycles for MgCl and $MgCl_2$ show that the latter system has the lower energy of the two. We have to find the enthalpy of formation of MgCl, that is ΔH_f for

$$Mg(s) \quad + \quad \tfrac{1}{2}Cl_2(g) \quad \rightarrow \quad MgCl(s)$$

The lattice enthalpy can be estimated; Na^+ and Mg^+ would be expected to be of similar size, so the crystal structure of MgCl and NaCl would be the same and ΔH_{latt} be similar too. Figures 1.5 and 1.6 show energy level diagrams for Born–Haber cycles relating to MgCl and $MgCl_2$, using the following data:

	$\Delta H^{\ominus}/$ kJ mol^{-1}
$Mg(s) \rightarrow Mg(g)$	$+150$
$Mg(g) \rightarrow Mg^+(g) + e^-$	$+736$
$Mg^+(g) \rightarrow Mg^{2+}(g) + e^-$	$+1450$
$Cl_2(g) \rightarrow 2Cl(g)$	$+242$

	$\Delta H^{\ominus}/$ kJ mol^{-1}
$Cl(g) + e^- \rightarrow Cl^-(g)$	-364
$Mg^+(g) + Cl^-(g) \rightarrow Mg^+Cl^-(s)$	-770
$Mg^{2+}(g) + 2Cl^-(g) \rightarrow Mg^+(Cl^-)_2(s)$	$^-2493$

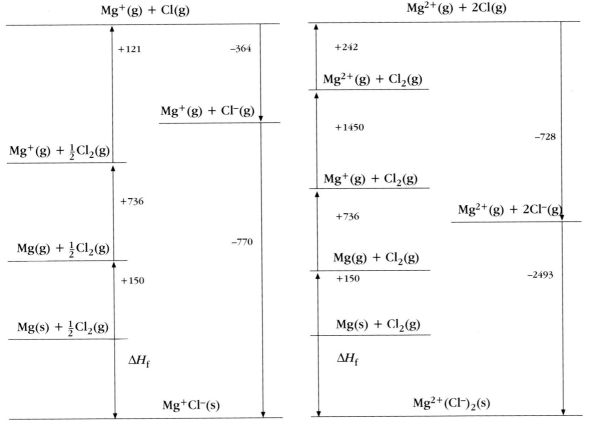

Figure. 1.5 The Born-Haber cycle for MgCl

Figure. 1.6. The Born-Haber cycle for MgCl₂

Applying Hess's law to the cycle in figure 1.5 gives:

$$\Delta H_f^{\ominus} (MgCl) = (+150) + (+736) + (+121) + (-364) + (-770)$$

whence $\Delta H_f^{\ominus} (MgCl) = -127$ kJ mol^{-1}.

Similarly for Figure 1.6, the calculation is:

$$\Delta H_f^{\ominus} (MgCl_2) =$$
$$(+150) + (+736) + (+1450) + (+242) + 2(-364) + (-2493)$$

$$\Delta H_f^{\ominus} (MgCl_2) = -643 \text{ kJ mol}^{-1}.$$

Both enthalpies of formation are exothermic, but the formation of $MgCl_2$ is more than twice as energetically favourable as MgCl. MgCl is never formed. The main factor which favours the formation of $MgCl_2$ is the very high lattice enthalpy. This more than compensates for the additional energy that has to be supplied for the second ionisation of magnesium.

Theoretical lattice enthalpies

An ionic crystal possesses only one lattice enthalpy, and that is the experimental value already mentioned. A real crystal like that of sodium chloride will not be fully ionic; there will always be some degree, even though it may be very little, of covalent bonding due to electron sharing. So it is instructive to compare the real lattice enthalpy obtained from a Born–Haber cycle with one calculated from a model where the crystal is considered to be completely ionic.

The calculation of the theoretical lattice enthalpy involves extending Coulomb's Law to three dimensions, considering repulsions as well as attractions and taking account of the crystal structure. Comparison of the theoretical lattice enthalpy with the experimental value gives a measure of the deviation of the crystal from the ionic model. This has already been mentioned in Chapter 3 of Module 1. The deviations, which make the crystal stronger than the ionic model predicts, give an indication of the contribution of covalent bonding. Deviations would be expected to be largest where the ions are small and of high charge, that is, the most polarising.

Changing the cation size

Table 1.3 shows the effect of changing the cation size on the difference between experimental (Born–Haber) and theoretical lattice enthalpies for the chlorides of Groups 1 and 2. Values are in kJ mol^{-1}.

Table 1.3 *Experimental (B-H) and theoretical lattice enthalpies for the chlorides of the s-block.*

	Cation radius/pm	Lattice enthalpy B–H	Lattice enthalpy theory		Cation radius/pm	Lattice enthalpy B–H	Lattice enthalpy theory
NaCl	102	−780	−770	MgCl$_2$	72	−2526	−2326
KCl	138	−711	−702	CaCl$_2$	100	−2258	−2223
RbCl	149	−685	−677	SrCl$_2$	113	−2156	−2127
CsCl	170	−661	−643	BaCl$_2$	136	−2056	−2033

Why do sodium chloride and caesium chloride have different crystal structures?

It would be expected that the greatest deviations from the ionic model would be for the smallest, most polarising cations. It is certainly true for MgCl$_2$ compared with the others. But how do we interpret the values for the Group 1 chlorides? The question really is, are they so very different? Bearing in mind that both the experimental and the theoretical values will have an error associated with them, in one case experimental error and in the other errors inherent in the theoretical model used, the evidence for these chlorides is that they are virtually completely ionic. Further, CsCl does not have the same crystal lattice as the others, and although this will have been taken into account in the calculation, the errors may very well not be the same.

If the anion size changes, we expect greater deviation from the ionic model with the larger, more polarizable anions. Iodides should therefore show greater differences than fluorides; table 1.4 shows that this is true. Values are in kJ mol^{-1}.

Table 1.4 *Theoretical and experimental lattice enthalpies for sodium and magnesium halides*

	Anion radius/pm	Lattice enthalpy B–H	Lattice enthalpy theory		Lattice enthalpy B–H	Lattice enthalpy theory
NaF	136	–918	–912	MgF$_2$	–2957	–2913
NaCl	181	–780	–770	MgCl$_2$	–2526	–2326
NaBr	195	–742	–735	MgBr$_2$	–2440	–2097
NaI	216	–705	–687	MgI$_2$	–2327	–1944

Lattice enthalpy and the solubility of ionic compounds

This material is part of topic 19, Groups 1 and 2 (chapter 4, page 46), but it fits well here.

A simple theory of solubility for ionic compounds, based solely on enthalpy changes, cannot be stated. This is because the solubility of most substances is not controlled by enthalpy changes alone, any more than the direction of spontaneous change is so controlled in chemical reactions (Module 2, Chapter 3). The problem cannot be examined generally without using the thermodynamic idea of entropy, and unfortunately quite small changes in entropy can have large consequences for solubility. This is beyond our present concerns, so we shall look only at compounds for which the enthalpy change of solution, ΔH_{soln}, is the governing factor.

When an ionic substance dissolves the enthalpy change depends upon

1 the lattice enthalpy, ΔH_{latt}, of the solid;

2 the hydration enthalpy, ΔH_{hyd}, of the ions.

ΔH_{hyd} is defined as the heat change per mole for the hydration of the gaseous ion with enough water for there to be no further heat change on dilution. For a unipositive cation ΔH_{hyd} is exothermic, for example:

$$M^+(g) + aq \rightarrow M^+(aq)$$

If it is roughly the same magnitude as ΔH_{latt}, or is greater, then the heat needed to break the lattice is recouped by the hydration of the ions and the dissolution of the solid is favoured.

In this case ΔH_{soln} is negative. A low solubility may be a consequence of high lattice enthalpy or a low hydration enthalpy of the ions.

The enthalpy changes for a salt M^+X^- can be represented on the Hess's Law cycle:

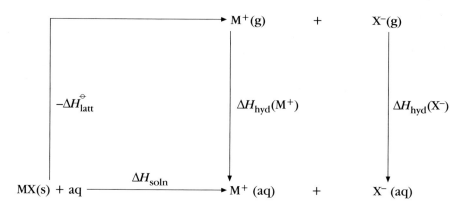

Figure 1.7 *Hess's Law cycle for the salt M^+X^-*

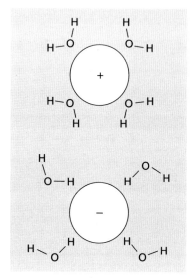

Figure 1.8 *The hydration of ions*

Find the enthalpy of solution of sodium chloride.

Data/kJ mol⁻¹:

Enthalpy of hydration of Na⁺   −406

Enthalpy of hydration of Cl⁻   −364

Lattice enthalpy of sodium chloride −771

From Hess's Law,

$$\Delta H_{soln} = \Delta H_{hyd}(M^+) + \Delta H_{hyd}(X^-) - \Delta H_{latt}(M^+X^-)$$

The hydration of ions occurs because the polar water molecules are attracted to the charge on the ion. The extent of the hydration depends on the charge density of the ion, that is its charge per unit surface area, so the higher the charge and the smaller the ion, the higher the hydration enthalpy will be.

Solubility trends in the hydroxides and sulphates of Group 2

Trends in solubility of a given type of compound for different metals in a group depend on which of the changes, in hydration enthalpy of the cation or in the lattice enthalpy of the compounds, are more important as the cation size increases down the group.

In the case of the sulphates of Group 2, the hydration enthalpy of the cation has most effect. The lattice enthalpy is partly a function of the sum of the radii of the cation and anion. The size of the sulphate ion is such that this quantity does not change very much as the cation size changes. Therefore the contribution from ΔH_{latt} is similar for all of the Group 2 sulphates. However, ΔH_{hyd} of the cations falls significantly as they get larger. Therefore the solubility of the sulphate falls with increasing cation size, because the lattice enthalpy is not exceeded so much by the hydration enthalpy.

Table 1.5. *Solubilities of group 2 sulphates and hydroxides*

			Sulphate	Hydroxide
Mg^{2+}	−1920	65	1.83×10^{-1}	2.00×10^{-5}
Ca^{2+}	−1650	99	4.66×10^{-3}	1.53×10^{-3}
Sr^{2+}	−1480	113	7.11×10^{-5}	3.37×10^{-3}
Ba^{2+}	−1360	135	9.43×10^{-7}	1.50×10^{-2}

In the case of the hydroxides, ΔH_{latt} is the more important factor. This is because the hydroxide ion is quite small, so the sum of the radii of the cation and the anion is significantly influenced by the cation size. This is seen clearly in the smaller differences in solubility for the hydroxides of the largest cations in group (Table 1.5). The lattice enthalpies of the hydroxides decrease as the cation gets larger since there is a poorer size match between the cation and the anion. ΔH_{latt} decreases more rapidly than the enthalpies of solvation.

Lattice enthalpies and thermal stability of carbonates and nitrates of the s-block.

This is also part of the content of topic 19.

Carbonates decompose on heating, and clear trends are evident. The decomposition of calcium carbonate is typical:

$$CaCO_3(s) \quad \rightarrow \quad CaO(s) \quad + \quad CO_2(g)$$

This reaction is important in cement manufacture and in the extraction of iron (Chapter 6, p72).

Since entropy considerations are more or less the same in each case, comparisons using enthalpy changes alone are quite accurate in these reactions.

The thermal stability of a carbonate will depend on the stability of the carbonate lattice compared with the oxide lattice at the same temperature. As the cation size changes, the lattice enthalpies of the carbonates and those of the oxides change by different factors. The lattice enthalpies of the carbonates change little, since the carbonate ion dominates in size. However the oxide lattice enthalpy falls faster as the cation size increases and there is a poorer size match between the big cations and the oxide ion. The thermal stabilities of group 2 carbonates decrease in the order

$$BaCO_3 \quad >> \quad SrCO_3 \quad > \quad CaCO_3 \quad > \quad MgCO_3 \quad >> \quad BeCO_3.$$

Barium carbonate does not decompose at Bunsen temperatures; all other Group 2 carbonates decompose in a similar way to calcium carbonate, according to the equation above. Beryllium carbonate decomposes at room temperature.

Group 1 cations are larger than those of group 2, and because of the smaller cation charge the lattice enthalpies of the carbonates are smaller too. The result of this is that the differences in lattice enthalpy between the carbonate and the oxide are not sufficient to allow the decomposition of the carbonates at normal Bunsen temperatures. The exception is lithium carbonate, which has the smallest cation; it decomposes to the oxide on heating.

An alternative view of the reasons for thermal decomposition is based on the polarising power of the cation. The larger the metal ion, the lower its polarising power because its charge density is less. Salts of large, polarisable anions, for example nitrate and carbonate, will be most stable with large, relatively non-polarising cations. Small polarising cations will favour small anions, since the lattice enthalpy will then be larger.

The nitrates illustrate these points further. Group 2 nitrates on heating all decompose to the metal oxide, brown nitrogen dioxide, and oxygen. Calcium nitrate is typical:

$$2Ca(NO_3)_2(s) \quad \rightarrow \quad 2CaO(s) \quad + \quad 4NO_2(g) \quad + \quad O_2(g)$$

The relatively small cations form stronger lattices with oxide than with the larger nitrate. The decomposition becomes more difficult as the cation size increases, barium nitrate requiring red heat.

In the case of Group 1, the larger cations result in reactions where the product is the nitrite. This is a smaller anion than nitrate, and so gives a higher lattice enthalpy than nitrates do. But it is not too small, which would be the case with the oxide.

$$2NaNO_3(s) \quad \rightarrow \quad 2NaNO_2(s) \quad + \quad O_2(g)$$

No brown gas is evolved. The nitrates are all white and the nitrites pale yellow.

Redox equilibria: the electrochemical cell

Redox reactions are those in which electrons are transferred; these have already been considered in Module 1, Chapter 4, Transition Metals, though redox reactions aren't exclusively confined to these metals by any means. In this chapter redox reactions are treated quantitatively, which enables the ordering of substances in terms of reactivity, the determination of the feasibility of a reaction and the calculation of the equilibrium constant. Technological applications of redox reactions in storage cells are also considered.

Some of this chapter is intended as extension material. Knowledge of this material helps in appreciating the significance of electrochemical cells, but it is not at present examinable in the London scheme. Such material is indicated as such in the text by an asterisk *.

Redox reactions and electrochemical cells

When zinc powder is added to a solution of copper(II) sulphate, the reaction which occurs is represented by:

$$Cu^{2+}(aq) \quad + \quad Zn(s) \quad \rightarrow \quad Cu(s) \quad + \quad Zn^{2+}(aq)$$

Electrons are transferred from the zinc metal to the copper ion, and the mixture becomes warm. This reaction can also be carried out in an electrochemical cell. The chemistry is the same, but the cell e.m.f. gives a measure of how likely the reaction is, since it is related to the equilibrium constant for the reaction. Such a measurement is made under conditions which do not draw current from the cell. With suitable engineering of the electrodes, current can be drawn, and the electrons can do work by moving along a wire to light a lamp or drive a motor on their way from the zinc to the copper ions. The reaction is that which is found in the Daniell Cell.

General principles of electrochemical cells

The Daniell Cell

This cell uses the simplest type of electrode, that is a metal dipping into a solution of its ions. The potential of the cell can be measured using the following arrangement in Figure 2.1

State carefully what you would see when excess zinc powder is stirred with a solution of copper(II) sulphate.

Find in each case the standard potentials of the cells obtained using the following electrodes; the data needed is in table 17.2. Write the equation in each case to represent the reaction which would occur if current were to be drawn from the cell.
(a) Fe^{2+}/Fe and Ni^{2+}/Ni;
(b) Al^{3+}/Al and Pb^{2+}/Pb;
(c) MnO_4^-/Mn^{2+} and I_2/I^-
(d) V^{3+}/V^{2+} and Fe^{3+}/Fe^{2+}
(e) $S_4O_6^{2-}/S_2O_3^{2-}$ and I_2/I^-.

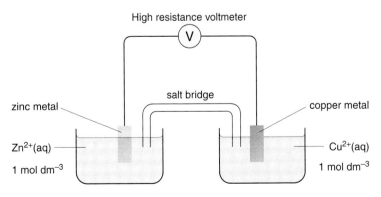

Figure 2.1 A Daniell cell

REDOX EQUILIBRIA: THE ELECTROCHEMICAL CELL

Figure 2.2 J. F. Daniell

The electrodes are connected to a voltmeter which has a very high resistance. This is to prevent any significant current from being drawn from the cell. A current would cause a voltage drop across the internal resistance of the cell, and the measured voltage would be less than the cell e.m.f.

The electrolyte solutions are connected by a salt bridge. This is usually a solution of potassium chloride in a U-tube, possibly set as a gel with agar. A strip of filter paper soaked in potassium chloride solution will serve as a simple version. If either of the metals used has an insoluble chloride, for example silver or lead, then potassium nitrate is used instead.

The salt bridge brings the two solutions into electrical contact. A wire cannot be used, since it would form two more electrodes, each with its own potential, where it dipped in to the two solutions. Further, if the cell is to be used as a source of power and current is drawn, ions have to move from one solution to the other, and ions cannot move through wires.

The origin of the cell potential

When a metal/metal ion electrode is set up, a potential arises because of the different environment of the metal ions in the two phases. The metal lattice consists of close-packed ions in a delocalised cloud of electrons, and the solution contains solvated metal ions. When the metal is dipped into the solution, two things can happen. The ions in the metal can leave the metal surface and enter the solution, the electrons remaining behind; and the ions in solution could become attached to the metal. In the first case the metal becomes negative with respect to the solution, in the second case positive. The equilibrium condition, when the two processes are happening at the same rate, is expressed by the reduction equation

$$M^{n+}(aq) \quad + \quad ne^- \quad \rightleftharpoons \quad M(s)$$

and the resulting potential is that which, together with the other electrode, produces electrochemical equilibrium for the ions in the different phases and hence the cell e.m.f.

The potential difference depends on the metal, on the temperature, and on the concentration of the solution. This potential cannot be measured.

A voltmeter is a two-terminal device which gives the potential difference between two points, and is connected to them by wires. One of these can be the metal of the electrode of interest, but the other connection to the solution will inevitably produce a metal immersed in ions – which is therefore another electrode, having its own potential. The only measurement which can be made is the difference between two electrode potentials; so that comparisons can be made between various electrodes, all are measured relative to a particular electrode. The standard hydrogen electrode is used, arbitrarily given a potential of zero (see opposite page).

State the reaction which would occur at the standard hydrogen electrode if it were combined with each of the following standard electrodes and current were to be drawn from the cell:

(a) Cu^{2+}/Cu;   (b) Zn^{2+}/Zn

The reaction between zinc and copper ions in an electrochemical cell gives a cell potential of 1.10V, which is the measurable difference between the unmeasurable individual electrode potentials of the two half cells.

Representing electrochemical cells

It is laborious to draw pictures of cells, so a shorthand representation is used. Phase boundaries are shown by vertical lines, and the salt bridge by a double dotted vertical line. The Daniell Cell is therefore represented as:

$$Zn(s) \mid Zn^{2+}(aq, 1 \text{ mol dm}^{-3}) \mathbin{\vdots\vdots} Cu^{2+}(aq, 1 \text{ mol dm}^{-3}) \mid Cu(s)$$

A common convention is that the *cell potential is positive if oxidation occurs at the left hand electrode*. An alternative view is that the sign of the right hand electrode's reduction potential gives the sign of the cell e.m.f.

The standard hydrogen electrode

This electrode is shown in Figure 2.2. It consists of a supply of hydrogen gas, and platinum coated in finely-divided platinum called platinum black. This is immersed in a solution of hydrogen ions. Provided that the platinum is in contact with both the gaseous and the aqueous phases, this arrangement allows the equilibrium

$$2H^+(aq) \;+\; 2e^- \;\rightleftharpoons\; H_2(g) \qquad E^{\ominus} \;=\; 0.00V \text{ defined}$$

to be set up. This behaves precisely as an electrode made from hydrogen would be expected to do.

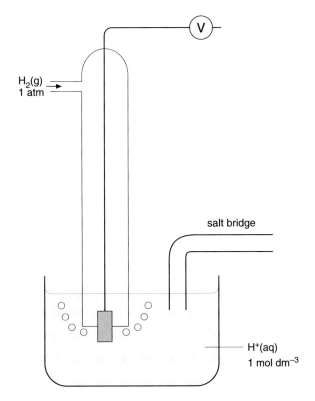

If the Daniell Cell
$Zn \mid Zn^{2+}(aq) \mathbin{\vdots} Cu^{2+}(aq) \mid Cu$
is set up under standard conditions, and an opposing potential greater than 1.10 V is applied to the terminals of the cell, what chemical changes would ensue?

Figure 2.3 The standard hydrogen electrode

REDOX EQUILIBRIA: THE ELECTROCHEMICAL CELL

Standard conditions
1 atm pressure
$[H^+]$ 1 mol dm^{-3}
stated temperature (298K)

Standard conditions are defined as being hydrogen at 1 atm pressure, $[H^+]$ of 1 mol dm^{-3}, and a stated temperature which is usually 298 K. Under these conditions this electrode has a defined potential of zero, and is used to define the standard electrode potential for other electrodes.

A temperature of 298 K is common for all thermodynamic measurements. Contrary to popular belief, this temperature does not form part of the definition of the thermodynamic standard state, which requires only a stated temperature.

The standard hydrogen electrode is not easy to set up accurately, so more convenient secondary electrodes are sometimes used. These have a potential defined in terms of the standard hydrogen electrode, but are not themselves primary standards.

The standard electrode potential $E^{\ominus}$

The standard electrode potential of any electrode is obtained by combining it with a standard hydrogen electrode, and measuring the potential of the cell produced. The standard conditions apply for both half cells. The arrangement for a metal/metal ion electrode is shown in figure 2.3.

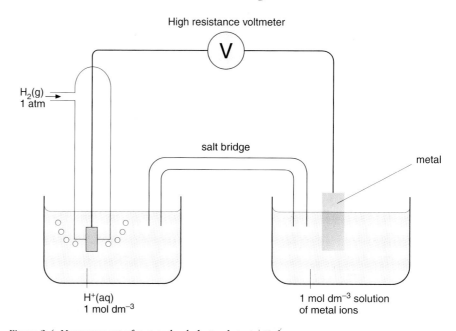

Figure 2.4 Measurement of a standard electrode potential

Accurate measurement of the cell potential requires a high resistance voltmeter so that that no current is drawn from the cell, otherwise there is a voltage drop across the internal resistance of the cell and the indicated potential is not the cell e.m.f.

The standard hydrogen electrode is conventionally drawn on the left-hand side in any diagram or representation of a cell. The potential of a cell is defined as

$$E_{cell} = E_{\text{right-hand electrode}} - E_{\text{left-hand electrode}}$$

where the potentials used are the reduction potentials. Consider the combination of the standard hydrogen electrode and a zinc/zinc ion electrode:

$$\text{Pt, H}_2 \text{ (1 atm)} \mid \text{H}^+ \text{ (aq, 1 mol dm}^{-3}) \mathbin{\vert\vert} \text{Zn}^{2+} \text{ (aq, 1 mol dm}^{-3}) \mid \text{Zn.}$$

The magnitude of the potential for this arrangement is 0.76V. However it has to be decided whether this is to be -0.76V or $+0.76$V. Given the convention mentioned above, that the cell potential is positive if oxidation occurs at the left-hand electrode, and knowing that in the equivalent test-tube reaction zinc is oxidised to zinc ions by dilute acids, the potential is defined as -0.76V. If current were to be drawn, reduction would occur at the hydrogen electrode according to

$$2\text{H}^+ \text{ (aq)} \quad + \quad 2e^- \quad \rightarrow \quad \text{H}_2\text{(g).}$$

If the hydrogen electrode were to be combined with a copper/copper ion electrode:

$$\text{Pt, H}_2 \mid \text{H}^+ \text{ (aq, 1 mol dm}^{-3}) \mathbin{\vert\vert} \text{Cu}^{2+} \text{ (aq, 1 mol dm}^{-3}) \mid \text{Cu}$$

the potential would be measured as $+0.34$ V. The positive sign can now be put in because it is found that electrons flow the opposite way to that with the zinc electrode, that is the connections to the voltmeter would have to have been reversed. If current were drawn the reaction at the hydrogen electrode would be

$$\text{H}_2 \text{ (g)} \quad \rightarrow \quad 2\text{H}^+ \text{ (aq)} + 2e^-.$$

It is because the standard hydrogen electrode not only determines the magnitude of the cell potential for other half cells, but also its sign, that it is conventionally drawn as the left-hand component.

For the Daniell Cell, the reduction potentials are

$$\text{Zn}^{2+}\text{(aq)} \quad + \quad 2e^- \quad \rightleftharpoons \quad \text{Zn(s)} \quad E^{\ominus} \quad = \quad -0.76 \text{ V}$$

$$\text{Cu}^{2+}\text{(aq)} \quad + \quad 2e^- \quad \rightleftharpoons \quad \text{Cu(s)} \quad E^{\ominus} \quad = \quad +0.34 \text{ V.}$$

The cell is represented

$$\text{Zn(s)} \mid \text{Zn}^{2+}\text{(aq, 1 mol dm}^{-3}) \mathbin{\vert\vert} \text{Cu}^{2+}\text{(aq, 1 mol dm}^{-3}) \mid \text{Cu(s)}$$

so that $E_{cell} \quad = \quad E_{\text{right-hand electrode}} - E_{\text{left-hand electrode}}$

$$= \quad +0.34 \text{ V} - (-0.76 \text{ V}) \quad = \quad +1.10 \text{ V}$$

The potential is positive, so zinc is oxidised to zinc ions. Always write the sign of a potential, positive or negative, to avoid any doubt as to what is meant.

REDOX EQUILIBRIA: THE ELECTROCHEMICAL CELL

The use of a standard electrode is similar to the use of mean sea level as the zero of height for maps; the stated height of a couple of mountains depends on where sea level is chosen to be. The difference in height between the two is the same, irrespective of sea level. The standard hydrogen electrode is used in the same way; whatever its actual, unmeasurable potential, that cancels out when two other standard potentials, both determined relative to the standard hydrogen electrode, are subtracted to get an overall cell potential. In the Daniell Cell, the cell potential is the difference between the potentials of zinc and copper electrodes, which is 1.10V. This will be the same no matter where the zero of measurement had been taken. Suppose that a fluorine electrode had been used as standard; then the copper electrode would have had a potential of –2.72V, that of zinc –3.82V ; and the difference would still be 1.10V.

Other types of electrode

The cation electrode (metal/metal ion) is not the only variety. Anion electrodes permit equilibria such as

$$Cl_2 \; + \; 2e^- \; \rightleftharpoons \; 2Cl^-$$

to be attained.

Oxidation–reduction electrodes have both the oxidised and reduced species in solution, electrical contact being made by a platinum electrode. One such electrode has MnO_4^-, Mn^{2+} and H^+ ions all at 1 mol dm^{-3} concentration, enabling the equilibrium

$$MnO_4^-(aq) \; + \; 8H^+(aq) \; + \; 5e^- \; \rightleftharpoons \; Mn^{2+}(aq) \; + \; 4H_2O(l)$$

to be set up.

Reversibility

Much has been made of the use of a high-resistance voltmeter so that current is not drawn from the cell. Under these conditions, there is no voltage drop across the internal resistance of the cell. Since no current is passing, that is no electrons are flowing, there is no chemical change at the electrodes either. Under such no-current conditions the electrodes are said to be **reversible**. What is being measured is the potential to do work, the electrical pressure (e.m.f.) which would be exerted on the electrons if they were allowed to flow. The idea of reversibility is quite subtle, but is important because it is only under reversible conditions that the true value of the electrode potential is obtained.

A reversible electrochemical cell is not at equilibrium; at equilibrium all possible net chemical reaction in the system has occurred, and the cell potential is zero. A cell or battery at equilibrium is flat, even though the equilibrium be dynamic; it has no potential to do work.

The meaning of the cell potential

Cell potential and the direction of spontaneous change

One of the uses of the cell potential is to determine whether a chemical reaction is thermodynamically favourable, that is whether it 'will go'. If the cell potential is positive for the reaction as written, then the reaction is thermodynamically favourable, and therefore spontaneous. In previous discussions of thermodynamics it has been necessary to include a caution whenever enthalpy changes alone have been discussed. A true picture can only be had if entropy changes are included too; you may recall this point having been made in the discussion of the solubility of ionic compounds in Module 1. Happily, conjectures made from $E^{\ominus}$ values include the entropy, so there is no problem. It is also necessary to consider the kinetics of the process if the reaction is to be used in practice; the electrode processes may have a high activation energy, and thus be very slow. Occasionally in examination answers comments are seen that a potential of between 0V and +0.3V does not give a feasible reaction. Maybe it wouldn't be fast, but if the cell potential is positive the reaction is thermodynamically feasible. Thermodynamics does not predict rates.

Non-standard conditions

The cell:

$$\text{Pt, Cl}_2 \text{ (1 atm)} \mid \text{Cl}^-\text{(aq, 1 mol dm}^{-3})\mathop{\vdots}\limits \text{Mn}^{2+}\text{(aq, 1 mol dm}^{-3}) \mid \text{MnO}_2, \text{Pt}$$

has a potential $E^{\ominus} \ = \ E^{\ominus}_{rhs} - E^{\ominus}_{lhs} \ = \ +1.23 - (+1.36)\text{V} = -0.13\text{V}.$

Therefore the reaction

$$\text{MnO}_2(s) + 4\text{HCl}(aq) \ \rightarrow \ \text{MnCl}_2(aq) + \text{Cl}_2(g) + 2\text{H}_2\text{O}(l)$$

is not thermodynamically favourable under standard conditions. Yet the reaction is that for the usual laboratory preparation of chlorine. The difference is that concentrated hydrochloric acid is used instead of acid at 1 mol dm^{-3}, and this changes the potentials sufficiently to enable the reaction to occur.

The cell potential of any reaction involving hydrogen ions will change if the pH changes. The oxidation of halide ions by manganate(VII) ions is therefore pH dependent. Calculations using electrode potentials show that under standard conditions MnO_4^- will oxidise Cl^-, Br^- and I^-; if the pH is raised to 3, the reduction potential of the $\text{MnO}_4^-/\text{Mn}^{2+}$ half-cell becomes less positive, and only Br^- and I^- are oxidised. At pH 5, only I– is.

The potential of a half cell becomes more positive as the concentration of the ions on the left hand side of the half reaction are increased. For the $\text{Cu}^{2+}|\text{Cu}$ half cell, a solution of concentration 10 mol dm^{-3} would give a potential of +0.37V compared with +0.34V. A similar change for $\text{Zn}^{2+}|\text{Zn}$ would change the potential from −0.76V to −0.73V

Caution is necessary, then, when deciding whether a reaction is possible based on standard electrode potentials. Changing the conditions can substantially affect the outcome.

Further significance of the cell potential

The four topics in this section are not at present examinable in the London scheme, but nevertheless are important aspects of electrochemistry. They are useful as a landscape in which to set the other material and relate it to other areas of chemistry.

The cell potential and the equilibrium constant*

The cell potential is directly related to the equilibrium constant for the cell reaction by the equation

$$\ln K_c = \frac{zFE^{\circ}_{cell}}{RT}$$

where z = number of electrons transferred in the cell reaction

F = Faraday constant = $96\ 484\ C\ mol^{-1}$

R = Gas constant = $8.314\ J\ K^{-1}\ mol^{-1}$

T = thermodynamic temperature, K

E°_{cell} = cell potential, V.

At 298 K the expression becomes

$$\ln K_c = zE^{\circ}_{cell}/0.0257$$

For the Daniell cell, where $E^{\circ}_{cell} = 1.10V$ and $z = 2$, $K_c = 1.5 \times 10^{37}$.

The reaction is complete!

Non-equilibrium electrochemistry*

A positive cell potential shows that a reaction is thermodynamically feasible. However, thermodynamics, that is the E° value, gives no idea of the rate of reaction. In order for a reaction to occur, the cell must produce current, where it is not operating reversibly. Considerations of kinetics at the electrode surfaces are then needed. This is left to much more advanced work. It must be realised here, though, that if the activation energy for the reaction is high, then it may well not happen at an observable rate, whatever E° might indicate.

The standard electrode potential and the ionisation energy*

Both of these quantities are related to the addition or the removal of electrons from an atom, so some relationship between them might be expected. Ionisation energy relates to the gas phase, and electrode potential to the aqueous phase, and it turns out that there are significant differences because of this.

Considering a Hess's Law cycle for the formation of aqueous ions of a divalent metal, we get

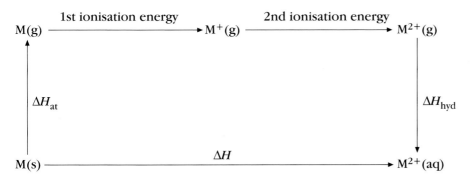

Figure 2.5 The Hess's Law cycle for the formation of aqueous ions of a divalent metal

In this diagram, $E°$ is related to, though is not identical with, ΔH. They are not exactly the same since $E°$ includes the entropy of the process. However, a comparison of the various values (Table 2.1) for copper and zinc, elements adjacent in the periodic table, suggests why the $E°$ values are very different even though the other quantities are similar.

Table 2.1 *Various enthalpy changes (in kJ mol^{-1}) for copper and zinc.*

	ΔH_{at}	ΔH_{ion} 1	ΔH_{ion} 2	ΔH_{hyd}	ΔH	$E°/V$
Cu	+338	+745	+1960	−2100	+943	+0.34
Zn	+131	+908	+1730	−2050	+719	−0.76

Making the reasonable assumption that the entropy changes are similar in each case, most of the difference between the behaviour of copper and zinc lies in the enthalpy of atomisation (the rest of the pathway differing by 17 kJ mol^{-1}); a property also reflected in the melting temperatures of these two metals: copper 1083 °C, zinc 420 °C. This in turn is related to the metallic radius: copper 128 pm, zinc 133 pm. We have an example of considerably different chemical properties for adjacent *d*-block metals arising from rather finely balanced differences in energies, a phenomenon alluded to in Module 1.

The pH meter*

The pH meter is an electrochemical cell, where everything except one of the electrolyte solutions is engineered into a single probe. Most pH meters have a reference electrode connected to the probe tip by a salt bridge, usually a thin thread moistened with potassium chloride, together with the pH-dependent electrode. This is made of high conductivity glass about 50 μm thick, containing a silver wire coated in silver chloride dipping in a mixture of phosphate buffer and potassium chloride. The test solution forms part of the glass electrode half cell whose potential depends on the pH, so the cell e.m.f. depends on the concentration of the hydrogen ions. The voltmeter is calibrated in pH units rather than volts. For reasons to do with the way the glass electrode works, pH meters are not very accurate at very low or very high pH. The meter is calibrated with a buffer of known pH in the range of interest before it is used. Some pH meters include a temperature compensating probe.

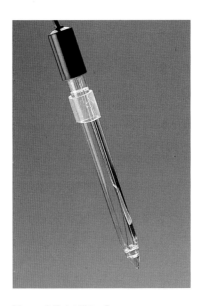

Figure 2.6 A pH probe

The glass electrode is one form of ion-sensitive electrode. There are others; the monitoring of water quality, for example, uses electrodes which are sensitive to dissolved oxygen, or to calcium ions.

Oxidation numbers and redox reactions

This material is similar to that covered in chapter 2 of Module 1, with some amplification concerning its relevance to electrochemical cells.

Oxidation numbers

For simple monatomic ions such as Fe^{2+} it's easy to see when they are oxidised (to Fe^{3+}) or reduced (to Fe). For ions such as NO_3^- or SO_3^{2-} which also undergo both oxidation and reduction it is not always so easy to see what is happening in terms of electrons. To assist this, the idea of oxidation number (or oxidation state) is used. The two terms are usually used interchangeably, so that an ion may have a particular oxidation number or be in a particular oxidation state.

Each element in a compound is treated as though it is an ion, no matter what the actual nature of the bonding; if during a reaction the 'charge' on the 'ion' becomes more positive, then that part of the compound has been oxidised. The inverted commas are used because the compound may not be ionic – it is taken to be so for this electronic book-keeping exercise.

Some atoms have defined oxidation states. There are three rules:

1. Elements have oxidation number of zero.

2. A simple monatomic ion has an oxidation number that is the same as its charge. The oxidation number is given in Arabic numerals with the appropriate sign, except when naming compounds where Roman numerals are used. Thus Fe^{3+} is iron($+3$), but a compound of it would be, say, iron(III) chloride.

3. In compounds the oxidation number of hydrogen is ($+1$), and that of oxygen is (-2) (there are some exceptions, considered later); fluorine is **always** (-1).

Consider the reaction between chlorine and bromide ions. The oxidation numbers are shown underneath each substance:

$$Cl_2 \text{ (aq)} \quad + \quad 2Br^-\text{(aq)} \quad \rightarrow \quad 2Cl^-\text{(aq)} \quad + \quad Br_2\text{(aq)}$$
$$(0) \quad\quad\quad\quad (-1) \quad\quad\quad\quad (-1) \quad\quad\quad (0)$$

The chlorine has been reduced because its oxidation number has gone down; the bromide ion has been oxidised because its oxidation number has risen.

REDOX EQUILIBRIA: THE ELECTROCHEMICAL CELL

That example is simple enough to make the use of oxidation numbers unnecessary in such a formal way. However, consider the reaction of manganate(VII) ions with iron(II) ions:

$$MnO_4^-(aq) + 5Fe^{2+}(aq) + 8H^+(aq)$$
$$\rightarrow Mn^{2+}(aq) + 5Fe^{3+}(aq) + 4H_2O(l).$$

Clearly the iron(II) ions have been oxidised to iron(III), but not so easy to see why there are 5 of them for every MnO_4^-. If we use the oxidation number, O is (-2), so pretending that the manganate ion is wholly ionically bonded we get:

$$[Mn^{x+}(O^{2-})_4]^-$$

from which $x = 7$. Thus since the product is Mn^{2+}, there must have been five electrons added to the MnO_4^- to reduce it. These come from 5 Fe^{2+} ions. The manganese in MnO_4^- is not actually a 7+ ion (indeed you will know from Module 1, Chapter 3 that such a highly-charged ion would be so polarising as to give covalent bonding) but it behaves in redox reactions as though it is.

Another common oxidising agent is dichromate(VI), $Cr_2O_7^{2-}$, which is not quite as powerful as manganate(VII). Using the same idea as before, in this case $[(Cr^{y+})_2(O^{2-})_7]^{2-}$, we get $y=6$. When dichromate(VI) is reduced, it forms two Cr^{3+} ions, a 6 electron change.

To see which part of a compound is negative and which is positive in finding oxidation numbers, the electronegativity is used. The more electronegative atom has the negative oxidation number. So in ammonia, NH_3, nitrogen is the more electronegative and has oxidation number (-3); in nitrite, NO_2^-, it is $(+3)$, and in nitrate, NO_3^-, $(+5)$. Carbon in carbon dioxide, CO_2 is $(+4)$, but in methane, CH_4, it is (-4). This is because carbon is more electronegative than hydrogen. The oxidation number is not the same as an element's valency or combining power. Carbon shows valency four only.

Sometimes hydrogen does not have oxidation number $(+1)$. In sodium hydride, NaH, it is combined with a less electronegative atom, and so hydrogen has oxidation number (-1) in ionic hydrides. Oxygen shows positive oxidation numbers only when combined with fluorine, e.g. it is $(+2)$ in oxygen difluoride OF_2.

Compounds or ions which apparently show fractional oxidation numbers usually have atoms of the same type with two or more different oxidation numbers. In tri-iron tetroxide, Fe_3O_4, for example, there is one $Fe(+2)$ and one $Fe(+3)$, the oxide behaving as $FeO.Fe_2O_3$. In trilead tetroxide, Pb_3O_4, the compound behaves as $2PbO.PbO_2$, i.e. as $Pb(+2)$ and $Pb(+4)$. The only exception to this idea is the superoxide ion O_2^-, with oxidation number for the oxygen of $(-1/2)$. The superoxide ion is a radical anion, having an unpaired electron.

A sample of cast iron weighing 0.5 g was converted to an acidified solution of iron(II) sulphate. This solution required 17.1 cm^3 of 0.01 mol dm^{-3} potassium manganate(VII) solution for complete oxidation. Find the percentage iron in the sample.

REDOX EQUILIBRIA: THE ELECTROCHEMICAL CELL

Oxidation numbers, redox reactions and the cell potential

The usefulness of oxidation numbers lies largely in the derivation of equations for redox reactions. The half-reactions that are combined are those which occur at each of the electrodes in the electrochemical cell. Knowing a few half-reactions means that you can combine them into a wide variety of full reactions since a particular oxidising agent is, under given conditions, often reduced in the same way whatever the reducing agent.

The oxidation of bromide ions by chlorine, mentioned earlier, affords a simple example. Chlorine is reduced to chloride ions:

$$Cl_2(aq) \ + \ 2e^- \ \rightarrow \ 2Cl^-(aq)$$

and bromide oxidised to bromine:

$$2Br^-(aq) \ \rightarrow \ Br_2(aq) \ + \ 2e^-.$$

Addition of these two half-reactions gives the full reaction

$$Cl_2(aq) \ + \ 2Br^-(aq) \ \rightarrow \ Br_2(aq) \ + \ 2Cl^-(aq).$$

The electrons given up by the bromide ions are the same electrons as those accepted by the chlorine atoms if the reaction is done in a test-tube. If an electrochemical cell is used, the electrons from the oxidised species will flow through the wire to the electrode where reduction occurs, and the left hand electrode will produce the same number of electrons that are used in the right hand electrode. Getting the number of electrons the same may require one or both half-reactions to be multiplied by an integer.

Manganate(VII) ion in acid solution is reduced to manganese(II), the half-reaction in acid solution being:

$$MnO_4^-(aq) \ + \ 8H^+(aq) \ + \ 5e^- \ \rightarrow \ Mn^{2+}(aq) \ + \ 4H_2O(l).$$

The half reaction for oxidation of iron(II) to iron(III) is:

$$Fe^{2+}(aq) \ \rightarrow \ Fe^{3+}(aq) \ + \ e^-$$

and since 5 electrons are needed to reduce the manganate(VII) this equation is multiplied by 5 and then added to the MnO_4^- half-reaction to get

$$MnO_4^-(aq) \ + \ 5Fe^{2+}(aq) \ + \ 8H^+(aq)$$
$$\rightarrow \ Mn^{2+}(aq) \ + \ 5Fe^{3+}(aq) \ + \ 8H_2O(l)$$

An important question concerns what should be done with the cell potential when the equations are so multiplied. The answer is, nothing should. Consider the half reactions again, this time including the cell potentials.

$$MnO_4^-(aq) + 5e^- + 8H^+(aq) \rightarrow Mn^{2+}(aq) + 4H_2O(l) \quad E^\circ = +1.51V$$

$$Fe^{2+}(aq) \rightarrow Fe^{3+}(aq) + e^- \quad E^\circ = -0.77V$$

The sign of the potential for the second equation has been reversed compared with that in your Data Book because the Data Book value is a reduction potential. By multiplying the second equation by 5 and adding, the overall reaction and the cell potential is obtained:

$$MnO_4^-(aq) + 5e^- + 8H^+(aq) \rightarrow Mn^{2+}(aq) + 4H_2O(l) \quad E^\circ = +1.51V$$

$$5Fe^{2+}(aq) \rightarrow 5Fe^{3+}(aq) + 5e^- \quad E^\circ = -0.77V$$

$$MnO_4^-(aq) + 5Fe^{2+}(aq) + 8H^+(aq)$$
$$\rightarrow Mn^{2+}(aq) + 5Fe^{3+}(aq) + 8H_2O(l) \quad E = +0.74V$$

The potential for the iron half-cell has not been altered. Thermodynamics makes a distinction between **extensive** properties which depend on the amount of material that is used, and **intensive** properties, which do not. Extensive properties include mass and volume; intensive ones include density, conductivity – and the reduction potential.

Earlier reference has been made to the dependence of the standard electrode potential on the concentration of the electrolyte and on the temperature. It does not depend on how much material is used to make the cell. The cell dealt with above is

$$Pt \mid Fe^{2+}, Fe^{3+}, (aq, 1 \text{ mol dm}^{-3}) \mid\mid MnO_4^-, Mn^{2+}(aq, 1 \text{ mol dm}^{-3}) \mid Pt$$

and it can be made using thimbles or buckets, without altering the value of the cell potential. The huge lead–acid batteries on a milk float have the same potential as the much smaller versions on a motor scooter. This also means that the area of the metal in the electrode does not affect the potential either.

The potential we have calculated is of course the reversible potential, the one obtained when no current is being drawn. If current is drawn, then the amount of electricity which the cell will provide depends on the amount of the chemicals it contains. This is the difference between cells of different size but of a given type; the larger one will provide more charge.

Redox titrations

A number of widely used titrations are redox processes. Potassium manganate(VII) can be used to titrate Fe^{2+}, NO_2^-, SO_3^{2-}, $C_2O_4^{2-}$, and H_2O_2. Sodium thiosulphate, $Na_2S_2O_3$, is used to titrate iodine which can be produced from a variety of other reactions.

REDOX EQUILIBRIA: THE ELECTROCHEMICAL CELL

A quantity of sodium ethanedioate was weighed out and dissolved in water to make 250cm^3 of solution. A 25.0cm^3 portion was acidified with dilute sulphuric acid, warmed to 60°C and titrated with 0.02 mol dm^{-3} potassium manganate(VII) solution; 27.3 cm^3 was required for complete oxidation. How much sodium ethanedioate was originally weighed out, assuming it to have been pure?

Potassium manganate(VII) titrations

Potassium manganate(VII) is an intensely purple substance, and gives a pink colour even in very dilute solution. It is its own indicator. It is usually used in the burette, so that the slight excess present in the reaction mixture when the endpoint is reached is easily seen as a pink coloration. The half reaction for its reduction in acidic solution, the usual conditions of use, is no doubt familiar by now:

$$MnO_4^-(aq) + 8H^+(aq) + 5e^- \rightarrow Mn^{2+}(aq) + 4H_2O(l). \quad E^\ominus = +1.51V$$

Potassium manganate(VII) is a strong oxidising agent and cannot be obtained in a high state of purity. It easily oxidises organic materials, say specks of dust present in the solutions, and these slowly deposit manganese(IV) oxide on standing. For these reasons, solutions cannot be made accurately by weighing the solid, so they must be standardised against a solution which can be so made (a primary standard). Sodium ethanedioate $Na_2C_2O_4$ is commonly used as a standard.

The reaction for the oxidation of ethanedioate ions is

$$C_2O_4^{2-}(aq) \rightarrow 2CO_2(g) + 2e^-$$

so the overall reaction is therefore

$$2MnO_4^-(aq) + 5C_2O_4^{2-}(aq) + 16H^+(aq)$$
$$\rightarrow 2Mn^{2+}(aq) + 10CO_2(g) + 8H_2O(l).$$

$E^\ominus_{cell}$ is +1.02 V. The potassium manganate(VII) solution is run into a standard solution of sodium ethanedioate at about 60°C; initially the reaction is quite slow, but as soon as some manganese(II) ion is produced this catalyses the reaction which becomes much faster. Such a reaction where the products catalyse the reaction is called **autocatalytic**.

A sample of sodium sulphite weighing 1.80 g was weighed out and made to 250 cm^3 of aqueous solution. 25.0 cm^3 portions of this were acidified with dilute sulphuric acid, and titrated with 0.02 mol dm^{-3} potassium manganate(VII) solution. 26.2 cm^3 was required for oxidation. Find the percentage purity of the sodium sulphite.

Potassium manganate(VII) in acidic solution oxidises nitrite, NO_2^-, to nitrate, NO_3^-, $E^\ominus_{cell} = +0.57V$; sulphite, SO_3^{2-} to sulphate, SO_4^{2-}, $E^\ominus_{cell} = +1.34V$; and Fe^{2+} to Fe^{3+}, $E^\ominus_{cell} = +0.74V$. It is used to analyse these materials titrimetrically.

Sodium thiosulphate titrations

Sodium thiosulphate is used to titrate iodine, which oxidises it to tetrathionate ions, $S_4O_6^{2-}$, whilst the iodine forms iodide ions:

$$2S_2O_3^{2-}(aq) + I_2(aq) \rightarrow S_4O_6^{2-}(aq) + 2I^-(aq). \quad E^\ominus_{cell} = +0.53 \text{ V}$$

The substance of analytical interest usually produces the iodine in another reaction by oxidation of iodide ions. Thus aqueous copper(II) will oxidise iodide ions:

$$2Cu^{2+}(aq) + 4I^-(aq) \rightarrow 2CuI(s) + I_2(aq) \quad E^\ominus_{cell} = +0.32 \text{ V}$$

so the liberated iodine can be titrated with sodium thiosulphate solution. This titration can be used to determine the amount of copper in brass, for example, or the number of molecules of water of crystallisation in hydrated copper(II) sulphate.

As titrations of iodine with thiosulphate ions proceed, the solution becomes pale yellow; at the endpoint it turns colourless (unless other coloured substances are present), but since this can be difficult to see, freshly prepared starch solution is often added near the endpoint. The solution turns deep blue-black due to a starch/iodine complex, which disappears at the endpoint.

Sodium thiosulphate is oxidised to sulphate ions by other halogens, but is not used for their analysis

Disproportionation and electrochemical cells

Disproportionation reactions involve simultaneous oxidation and reduction of an atom in a given species, so can only occur if this atom is in an intermediate oxidation state. If the cell potential for the disproportionation is positive, it is thermodynamically feasible.

The reaction of chlorine with dilute sodium hydroxide solution gives sodium chlorate(I) and sodium chloride:

$$Cl_2(g) + 2NaOH(aq) \rightarrow NaOCl(aq) + NaCl(aq) + H_2O(l).$$

Ionically:

$$Cl_2(g) + 2OH^-(aq) \rightarrow OCl^-(aq) + Cl^-(aq) + H_2O(l).$$

The half reactions for this process are

$$Cl_2(aq) + 2e^- \rightleftharpoons 2Cl^-(aq) \qquad\qquad E^\circ = +1.36 \text{ V}$$

$$OCl^-(aq) + H_2O(l) + e^- \rightleftharpoons Cl_2(aq) + 2OH^- \quad E^\circ = +0.89 \text{ V}$$

In this reaction chlorine is oxidised to chlorate(I), OCl^-, and reduced to chloride; E°cell = +0.47V. The reaction is feasible under standard conditions.

Now consider whether the disproportionation of manganese(IV) oxide is possible in acidic solution to give manganese(II) and manganate(VII) ions. The half reactions are

$$MnO_2(s) + 2e^- + 4H^+(aq) \rightleftharpoons Mn^{2+}(aq) + 2H_2O(l) \qquad E^\circ = +1.23 \text{ V}$$

$$MnO_4^-(aq) + 3e^- + 4H^+(aq) \rightleftharpoons MnO_2(s) + 2H_2O(l) \quad E^\circ = +1.70 \text{ V}$$

A 25.0 cm³ sample of dilute hydrochloric acid is treated with potassium iodate(V) and potassium iodide in sufficient quantity to liberate iodine and use up all the hydrogen ions available. The iodine was titrated with sodium thiosulphate solution of concentration 0.1 mol dm⁻³, 27.8 cm³ being required. Find the concentration in mol dm⁻³ of the hydrochloric acid.

A sample of a copper alloy weighing 2.83 g was treated so as to convert it to 250 cm³ of a neutral solution containing copper as copper(II) ions. 25.0 cm³ portions of this solution were treated with excess potassium iodide, and the liberated iodine titrated with 0.1 mol dm⁻³ sodium thiosulphate solution. 26.7 cm³ was required. Find the percentage by mass of the copper in the alloy.

Write equations to represent the reactions between chlorine and thiosulphate ions, and iodine and thiosulphate ions, and suggest reasons for the difference based on electrode potential data.

Use table 2.2 to show whether disproportionation will occur in the following cases under standard conditions:

(a) $VO^{2+} \rightarrow VO_2^+$ and V^{3+}
(b) $MnO_2 \rightarrow MnO_4^-$ and Mn^{2+}

Suitable combination of these half-equations gives the overall reaction

$$5MnO_2(s) + 4H^+(aq)$$
$$\rightarrow 3Mn^{2+}(aq) + 2MnO_4^-(aq) + 2H_2O(l) \qquad E^\circ cell = -0.47V$$

The reaction does not occur under standard conditions.

The electrochemical series

The ordering of elements into a reactivity series is difficult if ordinary test-tube reactions are used. It is not possible, for example, to distinguish the reactivity of lead and tin accurately, since both react rather slowly with, say, acids. In any case in these reactions the rate of reaction is used to assess reactivity, and what is needed is a thermodynamic measure of reactivity independent of kinetics.

The electrode potential is a suitable measure of reactivity in thermodynamic terms, and ordering reduction potentials according to size gives the electrochemical series. The most reactive metals are those with the most negative potentials, the most reactive non-metals have the most positive potentials. Table 2.2 gives part of the electrochemical series, that is reduction potentials in order.

The distinction between the electrochemical potential and the observed reactivity in the test-tube, that is the rate of the reaction, is illustrated well by a comparison of lithium and potassium. If added to water lithium reacts rather slowly to give lithium hydroxide and hydrogen:

$$2Li(s) + 2H_2O(l) \rightarrow 2LiOH(aq) + H_2(g)$$

The reaction is not violent; yet that of potassium with water is, and dangerous if anything other than a minute piece of potassium is used.

Corrosion

Corrosion is the conversion of a metal in its normal working environment, mostly iron in practice, to its ions. It is therefore oxidation, and many circumstances where corrosion occurs involve electrochemical cells.

Rusting

Rust is a hydrated iron oxide, $Fe_2O_3.xH_2O$, and is commercially one of the most significant compounds of iron. Enormous amounts of money are involved in preventing rusting and in replacing artefacts that have fallen victim to it.

Figure 2.7 Rusting – the remains of a car in an Australian scrapyard

Rusting requires oxygen and a film of *liquid* water on the iron. Water vapour is not enough, since the water film forms the electrolyte in which corrosion occurs.

Table 2.2. *Selected standard reduction potentials*

Reaction		$E^{\ominus}/V$
$Li^+(aq) + e^-$	$\rightleftharpoons$ $Li(s)$	-3.03
$Rb^+(aq) + e^-$	$\rightleftharpoons$ $Rb(s)$	-2.93
$K^+(aq) + e^-$	$\rightleftharpoons$ $K(s)$	-2.92
$Ca^{2+}(aq) + 2e^-$	$\rightleftharpoons$ $Ca(s)$	-2.87
$Na^+(aq) + e^-$	$\rightleftharpoons$ $Na(s)$	-2.71
$Mg^{2+}(aq) + 2e^-$	$\rightleftharpoons$ $Mg(s)$	-2.37
$Al^{3+}(aq) + 3e^-$	$\rightleftharpoons$ $Al(s)$	-1.66
$Zn^{2+}(aq) + 2e^-$	$\rightleftharpoons$ $Zn(s)$	-0.76
$Fe^{2+}(aq) + 2e^-$	$\rightleftharpoons$ $Fe(s)$	-0.44
$PbSO_4(s) + 2e^-$	$\rightleftharpoons$ $Pb(s) + SO_4^{2-}(aq)$	-0.36
$V^{3+}(aq) + e^-$	$\rightleftharpoons$ $V^{2+}(aq)$	-0.26
$Ni^{2+}(aq) + 2e^-$	$\rightleftharpoons$ $Ni(s)$	-0.25
$Pb^{2+}(aq) + 2e^-$	$\rightleftharpoons$ $Pb(s)$	-0.13
$\mathbf{2H^+(aq) + 2e^-}$	$\rightleftharpoons$ $\mathbf{H_2(g)}$	$\mathbf{0.00}$
$S_4O_6^{2-}(aq) + 2e^-$	$\rightleftharpoons$ $2S_2O_3^{2-}(aq)$	$+0.09$
$SO_4^{2-}(aq) + 4H^+(aq) + 4e^-$	$\rightleftharpoons$ $H_2SO_3(aq) + H_2O(l)$	$+0.17$
$Cu^{2+}(aq) + 2e^-$	$\rightleftharpoons$ $Cu(s)$	$+0.34$
$VO^{2+}(aq) + 2H^+(aq) + e^-$	$\rightleftharpoons$ $V^{3+}(aq) + H_2O(l)$	$+0.34$
$IO^-(aq) + H_2O(l) + e^-$	$\rightleftharpoons$ $I^-(aq) + 2OH^-(aq)$	$+0.49$
$I_2(aq) + 2e^-$	$\rightleftharpoons$ $2I^-(aq)$	$+0.54$
$Fe^{3+}(aq) + e^-$	$\rightleftharpoons$ $Fe^{2+}(aq)$	$+0.77$
$Ag^+(aq) + e^-$	$\rightleftharpoons$ $Ag(s)$	$+0.80$
$ClO^-(aq) + H_2O(l) + e^-$	$\rightleftharpoons$ $Cl^-(aq) + 2OH^-(aq)$	$+0.89$
$NO_3^-(aq) + 3H^+(aq) + 2e^-$	$\rightleftharpoons$ $HNO_2(aq) + H_2O(l)$	$+0.94$
$VO_2^+(aq) + 2H^+(aq) + e^-$	$\rightleftharpoons$ $VO^{2+}(aq) + H_2O(l)$	$+1.00$
$Br_2(aq) + 2e^-$	$\rightleftharpoons$ $2Br^-(aq)$	$+1.09$
$MnO_2(s) + 4H^+(aq) + 2e^-$	$\rightleftharpoons$ $Mn^{2+}(aq) + 2H_2O(l)$	$+1.23$
$Cr_2O_7^{2-}(aq) + 14H^+(aq) + 6e^-$	$\rightleftharpoons$ $2Cr^{3+}(aq) + 7H_2O(l)$	$+1.33$
$Cl_2(aq) + 2e^-$	$\rightleftharpoons$ $2Cl^-(aq)$	$+1.36$
$PbO_2(s) + 4H^+(aq) + 2e^-$	$\rightleftharpoons$ $Pb^{2+}(aq) + 2H_2O(l)$	$+1.46$
$MnO_4^-(aq) + 8H^+(aq) + 5e^-$	$\rightleftharpoons$ $Mn^{2+}(aq) + 4H_2O(l)$	$+1.51$
$PbO_2(s) + SO_4^{2-}(aq) + 4H^+(aq) + 2e^-$	$\rightleftharpoons$ $PbSO_4(s) + 2H_2O(l)$	$+1.69$
$F_2(g) + 2e^-$	$\rightleftharpoons$ $2F^-(aq)$	$+2.87$
$F_2(g) + 2H^+(aq) + 2e^-$	$\rightleftharpoons$ $2HF(aq)$	$+3.06$

The process is shown in Figure 2.8.

A cell is formed between an area of iron and one of impurity, or an area where the metal has been stressed by working during manufacture. The anode reaction at the iron surface is

$$Fe(s) \rightarrow Fe^{2+}(aq) + 2e^-$$

the iron(II) ions then being oxidised to iron(III) ions by oxygen dissolved in the water. The electrons pass through the metal to the cathode area, where they reduce hydrogen ions in the water to hydrogen gas. The overall cell reaction is:

$$4Fe(s) + 3O_2(g) + 6H_2O(l) \rightarrow 4Fe(OH)_3(s) \equiv 2Fe_2O_3.xH_2O.$$

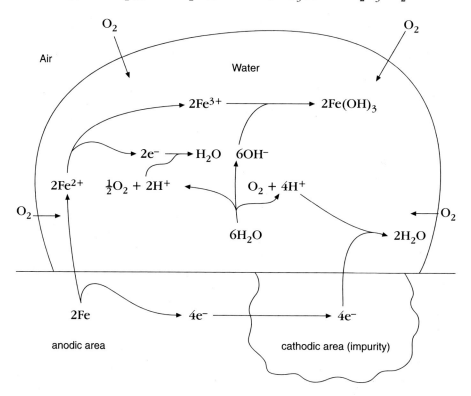

Figure 2.8 Rusting

Rust is hydrated iron oxide of variable composition. It flakes off the iron surface, exposing fresh metal to attack. If the water contains dissolved acid or salt, rusting is faster than with water alone; the electrolyte conductivity is increased, and the presence of other ions alters the electrode potentials. In some cases this is because of the formation of complexes of iron ions other than the aqua complexes $[Fe(H_2O)_6]^{2+}$ or $[Fe(H_2O)_6]^{3+}$ (Module 1, Chapter 4,).

Very pure iron, such as wrought iron, is resistant to rusting since cathodic areas are rare.

Corrosion of other metals

Although rusting is quantititatively the most significant form of corrosion, aluminium and magnesium alloys used in aircraft and ships will corrode. Corrosion is often found where two different metals are in contact, for example aluminium alloys riveted with magnesium alloy rivets, which forms a magnesium–aluminium cell ($E^° = +0.71V$), or steel bolts used with alloy components. Such corrosion is kept at bay by suitable maintenance and protection using various water-repellent materials as well as frequent cleaning and painting.

Sacrificial protection

Electrochemistry can be exploited in the prevention of rusting, as well as being the cause of it. A more reactive metal in contact with iron will corrode preferentially. This is used in galvanising, where the object is dipped in molten zinc. If the zinc coating is damaged, a cell is formed and the zinc will oxidise rather than the iron.

Ships and underground pipes, both occupying wet and salty environments, are protected by blocks of zinc or, more usually, magnesium, attached at intervals to the steel. These blocks corrode instead of the steel, and are replaced when necessary.

In these cases the intent is that the more reactive metal is sacrificed to preserve the steel, hence its being called a sacrificial coating.

Tinning

Zinc cannot be used to protect steel items used to contain foodstuffs. Although needed in small quantities for health, large amounts of zinc are toxic. Steel is therefore coated with tin instead. Tin is less reactive than iron ($E^° = -0.14V$) so it does not act as a sacrificial coat if it is damaged. Under such conditions, the iron does corrode. The purpose of the tin is simply to protect the iron with a tough, malleable, non-toxic coating. The preservation of food in 'tins' marked a dramatic advance in public health and food safety in the 19th century.

Concentration cells*

Consideration of corrosion is incomplete without brief reference to concentration cells, though these are not at present examinable in the London scheme. Since the potential of any electrode depends on the concentration of the electrolyte, it follows that a cell can be made from two identical metals if the concentration of the electrolytes differ. Such cells do not produce spectacular potentials; the cell

$$\text{Fe} \mid \text{Fe}^{2+}(\text{aq, 1 mol dm}^{-3}) \mid\mid \text{Fe}^{2+}(\text{aq, 0.1 mol dm}^{-3}) \mid \text{Fe}$$

has a potential of around 29 mV, for example. But considerable tonnages of iron are corroded because the oxygen concentration varies throughout a water

Figure 2.9 Tinning, the process of coating steel cans with tin, prevents corrosion and poses no risk to health

An acquaintance of the author once wished to make a vertical radio aerial consisting of a copper tube joined to the top of an aluminium tube. Give an electrochemical argument to dissuade him from this course of action.

film in contact with it, and this causes a variation in the potential of the oxygen half-cell involved in rusting. A concentration cell is formed, which might not make iron corrode very quickly, but does it very effectively. Such variations of oxygen concentration can arise at the edge of chips in a paint coating, or in cracks produced by working a metal or in crevices where two surfaces are bolted or riveted together.

Storage cells

Electrical energy is difficult to store. Electricity as such, that is charge, is stored in capacitors, but significant storage requires extremely large capacitors. Cells or batteries are stores of chemical energy which can be converted into electrical energy via redox reactions. All of the chemicals are contained within the cell; fuel cells, in contrast, use an external supply of chemical material.

The principal difference between storage cells and the reversible ones we have studied above is that storage cells must produce current, sometimes quite powerful current, and in many applications must be transportable without leakage. The problems of converting cells from a bench-top arrangement to safe, non-leaky portable cells suitable for mass production are largely technological, but the usable reactions are also limited by these factors.

The negative pole of a storage cell is that which produces electrons; the positive pole is that which accepts them.

The lead–acid cell

This cell, which was one of the first available for domestic use, is found in every motor vehicle. Its principal advantages are that it can produce powerful currents, for example when starting the engine in a car, and it is rechargeable. It is heavy and contains sulphuric acid, but neither feature is a problem in motor vehicles unless the cells are the principal power source, for example in milk floats.

The anode is made from lead and the cathode from lead(IV) oxide. These are immersed in dilute sulphuric acid. The reactions as the cell discharges are:

negative pole (anode):
$$Pb(s) + SO_4^{2-}(aq) \rightarrow PbSO_4(s) + 2e^- \qquad E^\ominus = -0.36V$$

positive pole (cathode):
$$PbO_2(s) + SO_4^{2-}(aq) + 4H^+ + 2e^- \rightarrow PbSO_4(s) + 2H_2O(i) \qquad E^\ominus = +1.69V$$

The cell reaction on discharge is:

$$Pb(s) + PbO_2(s) + 4H^+(aq) + 2SO_4^{2-}(aq) \rightarrow 2PbSO_4(s)$$

$$E^\ominus cell = +1.69 - (-0.36)V = 2.05V$$

At the anode, lead is oxidised to lead(+2), at the cathode lead(+4) is reduced to lead(+2). The electrodes, which are made from porous solids, both become lead(II) sulphate when the cell is completely discharged. Discharge removes sulphate ions from the electrolyte, which becomes less concentrated in sulphuric acid, and so its density falls. Charging from an external power supply (which might be the vehicle's alternator), reverses the reactions above. The charge condition of a lead/acid battery can be checked by finding the density of the electrolyte.

The 'zinc–carbon' cell

This cell is important since it was, until the advent of the high-capacity alkaline cell, the only so-called 'dry' battery. It has a potential of 1.5V. The zinc case of the cell is the anode; the electrolyte is a paste of ammonium chloride; the cathode is a graphite rod surrounded by a paste of ammonium chloride, powdered graphite and manganese(IV) oxide. The reactions are

negative pole: $Zn(s) \rightarrow Zn^{2+}(aq) + 2e^-$

positive pole: $2NH_4^+(aq) + 2e^- \rightarrow 2NH_3(aq) + H_2(g)$

Figure 2.10 A Leclanché cell

The hydrogen liberated would, if nothing were done to prevent it, coat the carbon; the cell is then said to be polarised and the voltage falls. The purpose of the manganese(IV) oxide is to prevent this from happening:

$$2MnO_2(s) + 3H_2(g) \rightarrow 2MnO(OH)(s) + 2H_2O(l).$$

The manganese compound is one of manganese(III). Ammonia is not liberated, but complexes with zinc ions fron the anode:

$$Zn^{2+}(aq) + 4NH_3(aq) \rightarrow [Zn(NH_3)_4]^{2+}(aq)$$

The reactions are not reversible, so the cell is not rechargeable – indeed it can explode if recharging is attempted, owing to gases being liberated. The Leclanché cell was the 'wet' precursor of the zinc-carbon cell.

The nickel-cadmium cell

The rechargeable NiCd cell is widely available in the same sizes as other, non-rechargeable cells. The electrodes are of nickel coated with nickel hydroxide, and cadmium coated with cadmium hydroxide, the electrolyte being aqueous sodium hydroxide. The reactions are

negative pole: $Ni(s) + 2OH^-(aq) \rightarrow Ni(OH)_2(s) + 2e^-$

positive pole: $Cd(OH)_2(s) + 2e^- \rightarrow Cd(s) + 2OH^-(aq)$

The cell has successfully been engineered to look and behave like any other, despite a number of disadvantages. Cadmium is very toxic, and the electrolyte is caustic; the cell potential is 1.1V rather than the 1.5V provided by zinc–carbon or alkaline cells. The cell e.m.f. falls at low temperature, so use of NiCd cells in radio equipment for expeditions, say, can be a problem if cold conditions are encountered. However cells can be recharged several hundred times.

3 | Gaseous and heterogeneous equilibria

Gaseous equilibria

Many equilibrium reactions exist which involve only gases. In such systems the concentration of the gases in moles per cubic decimetre can be used to find a value for the equilibrium constant K_c in the way which has been covered already in Module 2 Chapter 3. Nevertheless it is more convenient to measure the concentrations of gases in a mixture using the partial pressure of each of the gases.

Partial pressure

When a gas occupies a container of fixed volume at a given temperature, the pressure which is exerted by the gas depends only on the number of moles of gas present. The nature of the gas is not important. Under these conditions,

Pressure exerted by the gas α number of moles of the gas.

Thus:

n moles of oxygen	n moles of hydrogen	$2n$ moles of hydrogen
Pressure P.	The pressure is also P.	The pressure is now $2P$.

The gas pressure P can be measured in any convenient units; atmospheres (atm) are commonly used in chemistry, but the use of kN m^{-2} (kPa) will also be encountered in examination questions.

Since the pressure of the gas is independent of the nature of the gas, then a mixture of gases will also exert a pressure which depends only on the number of moles of gas:

$2n$ moles of oxygen	n moles of O_2 + n moles N_2
Pressure $2P$.	The pressure is also $2P$.

In such a mixture of gases, each gas exerts a **partial pressure** p. This is the pressure that the gas would exert if it alone filled the container, at a given temperature. The sum of the partial pressures of each gas in a mixture equals the total pressure in the container; this is Dalton's Law. Thus in the mixture of oxygen and nitrogen, the oxygen exerts a pressure P and the nitrogen also exerts a pressure P.

The principle that applies to any gas mixture uses the **mole fraction** of the gas, y. The mole fraction of a gas G, y_G, is defined:

$$y_G = \frac{\text{number of moles of gas G}}{\text{total number of moles of gas in the system}}$$

Dalton's Law
The sum of the partial pressure of each gas in a mixture equals the total pressure in the container.

If the mole fraction of each of the gases is known, together with the total pressure P_t, the partial pressure of each of the gases can be found. Each gas exerts a pressure which is this same fraction of the total pressure:

$$\text{Partial pressure of a gas} = \text{mole fraction} \times \text{total pressure}$$

$$p_G = y_G \times P_t$$

Partial pressures are therefore proportional to the number of moles of gas and are used as a measure of concentration in gas mixtures.

Calculate the mole fraction of each component in the following mixtures:

(a) 1.6 mol of nitrogen and 0.4 mol of oxygen;

(b) 0.5 mol of nitrogen, 0.7 mol of hydrogen, and 0.8 mol of ammonia.

Example 1

Thus in the equimolar mixture of nitrogen and oxygen considered initially:

$$\text{mole fraction of oxygen} = \frac{\text{number of moles of } O_2}{\text{number of moles of } O_2 + N_2}$$

$$= \frac{n}{n+n}$$

$$= \tfrac{1}{2}$$

Calculate the partial pressures of each of the gases in the preceding question if the total pressures are

(a) 2 atm   (b) 500 kN m^{-2}.

The mole fraction of nitrogen is clearly the same. Thus the partial pressures of oxygen and nitrogen are both given by:

$$p_{O_2} = p_{N_2} = \tfrac{1}{2} \times 2P = P.$$

Example 2

Now consider a mixture of nN_2 moles of nitrogen, nO_2 moles of oxygen and nCO_2 moles of carbon dioxide, in a container at a total pressure P_t. The total number of moles of gas present is

Thus:

$$n_{N_2} + n_{O_2} + n_{CO_2}$$

$$y_{N_2} = \frac{n_{N_2}}{n_{N_2} + n_{O_2} + n_{CO_2}} \quad \text{and}$$

$$y_{O_2} = \frac{n_{O_2}}{n_{N_2} + n_{O_2} + n_{CO_2}} \quad \text{and}$$

$$y_{CO_2} = \frac{n_{CO_2}}{n_{N_2} + n_{O_2} + n_{CO_2}}$$

and

$$p_{N_2} = y_{N_2}P_t, \quad \text{and} \quad p_{O_2} = y_{O_2}P_t \quad \text{and} \quad p_{CO_2} = y_{CO_2}P_t$$

Suppose that a vessel contains 1 mole N_2, 1 mole O_2 and 3 moles CO_2 at a total pressure of 7 atm. The total number of moles of gas is 5. By substituting in the equations above:

$$y_{N_2} = \tfrac{1}{5} \qquad\qquad y_{O_2} = \tfrac{1}{5} \qquad\qquad y_{CO_2} = \tfrac{3}{5}$$

and

$$p_{N_2} = \tfrac{1}{5} \times 7\text{atm} = 1.40 \text{ atm,}$$

$$p_{O_2} = \tfrac{1}{5} \times 7\text{atm} = 1.40 \text{ atm,}$$

$$p_{CO_2} = \tfrac{3}{5} \times 7\text{atm} = 4.20 \text{ atm.}$$

In calculations such as this you should always check that the sum of the partial pressures is the same as the given total pressure.

The equilibrium constant in terms of partial pressures

The composition of a gaseous reaction mixture which has reached a state of dynamic equilibrium at a given temperature is determined by the equilibrium constant. Each of the gases in the mixture will exert a partial pressure as shown above. The equilibrium composition and hence the equilibrium constant can be defined in terms of these partial pressures rather than the molar concentrations used for K_c. Consider for example the reaction between nitrogen gas and hydrogen gas, used in the Haber process to produce ammonia:

$$N_2(g) + 3H_2(g) \rightleftharpoons 2NH_3(g)$$

If the total equilibrium pressure is P_t, and the partial pressures of the individual gases in the equilibrium mixture are P_{N_2}, P_{H_2} and P_{NH_3} respectively, then the equilibrium constant in terms of partial pressures, K_p, is given by the expression:

$$K_p = \frac{(P_{NH_3})^2}{(P_{H_2})^3 (P_{N_2})} \qquad\qquad \text{The units are pressure}^{-2}.$$

The partial pressures are treated in exactly the same way as concentrations, so they are raised to a power according to the number of moles of gas in the equation for the reaction. The value of K_p describes the position of equilibrium and the concentrations of gases that can co-exist in an equilibrium. It does not generally have the same numerical value as K_c.

At a given temperature a mixture of nitrogen and hydrogen, initially mixed in a 1:3 molar ratio, gives an equilibrium mixture containing 12% of ammonia at 5 atm total pressure.

(a) Find the equilibrium constant for the reaction
$N_2(g) + 3H_2(g) \rightleftharpoons 2NH_3(g)$
at that temperature.

(b) Raising the temperature of the equilibrium mixture by 200 K gives a new equilibrium constant of 1.00×10^{-6} atm^{-1} at the same total pressure. State with reasons whether the forward reaction is exo- or endothermic.

At a certain temperature and at 10 atm total pressure a sample of dinitrogen tetroxide is 30% dissociated. Find the equilibrium constant for the reaction

$N_2O_4(g) \rightleftharpoons 2NO_2(g)$

under these conditions.

Gaseous dissociation

Thermal dissociation is the reversible breakdown of a substance into simpler substances on heating. It results in an equilibrium mixture. One such reaction is the dissociation of dinitrogen tetroxide into nitrogen dioxide:

$$N_2O_4(g) \rightleftharpoons 2NO_2(g)$$

and this will be used to illustrate the foregoing principles.

The extent of such a dissociation can be given in terms of the percentage dissociation. Thus if we started with 100 mol dinitrogen tetroxide which is 20% dissociated at equilibrium at a given temperature, there would be 80 mol left at equilibrium. The other 20 mol would have been converted to 40 mol of nitrogen dioxide. The equation shows that twice as many moles of NO_2 are formed from a given number of moles of N_2O_4. Putting the numbers of moles under the appropriate species in the equation, we have:

	$N_2O_4(g)$	$\rightleftharpoons$	$2NO_2(g)$
Numbers of moles initially:	100		0
Numbers of moles at equilibrium:	100 − 20		40

Total number of moles of gas at equilibrium $= 100 - 20 + 40 = 120$

Therefore: $y_{N_2O_4} = \dfrac{80}{120} = 0.667$ and $y_{NO_2} = \dfrac{40}{120} = 0.333$

If the total equilibrium pressure is P_t, then the partial pressures are:

$$p_{N_2O_4} = 0.667 \times P_t \quad \text{and} \quad p_{NO_2} = 0.333 \times P_t.$$

Now the value of K_p at this temperature can be calculated:

$$K_p = \frac{(0.333 \times P_t)^2}{0.667 \times P_t} = 0.166 P_t.$$

Instead of the percentage dissociation, the degree of dissociation α of a gas is frequently used. This is the fraction of the gas originally present that has dissociated. It is the percentage dissociation divided by 100 and is a fraction between 0 and 1. The degree of dissociation corresponding to 20% dissociation used in the example above is therefore 0.2.

GASEOUS AND HETEROGENEOUS EQUILIBRIA

At 1000 K, the equilibrium constant for the reaction

$H_2O(g) + C(s) \rightleftharpoons H_2(g) + CO(g)$

is 3.72 atm. Find the equilibrium partial pressures of each of the gases in the equilibrium mixture if the total pressure is 25 atm.

The advantage in using the degree of dissociation to find the position of equilibrium is that the initial number of moles of N_2O_4 need not be known. It is as if the initial number of moles is 1.00. Consider again the dinitrogen tetroxide/nitrogen dioxide equilibrium:

$$N_2O_4(g) \rightleftharpoons 2NO_2(g)$$

	$N_2O_4(g)$	$2NO_2(g)$
Initially:	1	0
At equilibrium:	$1 - \alpha$	2α

Total: $\quad 1 - \alpha + 2\alpha = 1 + \alpha$

Therefore: $\quad y_{N_2O_4} = \dfrac{1 - \alpha}{(1 + \alpha)} \qquad y_{NO_2} = \dfrac{2\alpha}{(1 + \alpha)}$

If the gas is 20% dissociated at the given temperature, $a = 0.2$.

Therefore: $\quad y_{N_2O_4} = \dfrac{0.8}{1.2} = 0.667$ and $y_{NO_2} = \dfrac{0.4}{1.2} = 0.333$.

The remainder of the calculation is as before.

Heterogeneous equilibria

If calcium carbonate is heated to a sufficient temperature, it decomposes to calcium oxide and carbon dioxide. In an open vessel, such as a test-tube, a blast furnace, or a lime-kiln, the carbon dioxide is lost and the reaction goes to completion. However, in a closed vessel the reaction is an equilibrium:

$$CaCO_3(s) \rightleftharpoons CaO(s) + CO_2(g)$$

Using the principles already covered, we can write a theoretical equilibrium constant for this reaction:

$$K_{c, \text{theor}} = \frac{[CaO][CO_2]}{[CaCO_3]}$$

the concentrations being those at equilibrium, and at constant temperature. What is meant, though, by the concentration of a solid? The concentration of a pure solid is the number of moles divided by its volume. It is no different from any other concentration – except that, since a pure solid has a constant density, it also has a constant concentration. Provided that there is some discrete calcium carbonate and some calcium oxide present in the system, that is it does not form a solid solution, the concentration of each is constant. The equation for $K_{c, \text{theor}}$ can therefore be rewritten

$$K_{c, \text{theor}} \times \frac{[CaCO_3]}{[CaO]} = [CO_2]$$

But the left hand side of this equation is a constant; this leads to the result that

$$K_{c, theor} \frac{[CaCO_3]}{[CaO]} = [CO_2] = K_c$$

Bringing the main points together: for the heterogeneous equilibrium

$$CaCO_3(s) \rightleftharpoons CaO(s) + CO_2(g)$$

$$K_c = [CO_2].$$

The general result is that, in expressions for K_c for heterogeneous equilibria, the solids are omitted from the expression. This is also true for K_p; for the same equilibrium,

$$K_p = p(CO_2).$$

A heterogeneous equilibrium which was at one time used to manufacture hydrogen is the reaction between iron and steam:

$$3Fe(s) + 4H_2O(g) \rightleftharpoons Fe_3O_4(s) + 4H_2(g)$$

The general rules we now have for K enable us to write

$$K_c = \frac{[H_2]^4}{[H_2O]^4}$$

$$\text{and } K_p = \frac{p_{H_2}{}^4}{p_{H_2O}{}^4}$$

QUESTION

State the effect of doubling the partial pressure of carbon monoxide on the equilibrium mixture

$$Ni(s) + 4CO(g) \rightleftharpoons Ni(CO)_4(g).$$

4 Groups 1 and 2

The s–block elements

Groups 1 and 2 of the Periodic Table are called the s-block elements since the outer electrons are in s orbitals. Group 1 elements are also called the alkali metals and Group 2 elements the alkaline earth metals. The two groups have fairly simple chemistries with clear trends, and are metals which are very reactive and of very low density when compared with metals as a whole. The compounds of both groups are almost wholly ionic, the Group 1 and 2 metals having oxidation numbers of +1 and +2 respectively. They have no other oxidation states. The compounds are usually colourless unless a transition metal is present in the anion, for example potassium manganate(VII), $KMnO_4$ is purple owing to the purple MnO^{4-} ion; or in the special case of superoxides, covered later.

Inorganic chemistry of metals typically deals with their reactions with oxygen and water, since these are abundant naturally, and with chlorine, being a strong oxidising agent.

The elements

Draw (small) graphs of the data in table 4.1 vs atomic number.

Group 1

Compared with the metals of the d-block, the alkali metals are not very dense, and have low melting and boiling temperatures; these properties are given in Table 4.1. The metals are soft, and can easily be cut with a knife, potassium being roughly the texture of plasticine. The abundance of each element in the Earth's crust is given in parts per million; only sodium and potassium are common.

Table 4.1 *Some physical properties of Group 1 elements.*

Element	Atomic radius/pm	Ionic radius/pm	Density g/cm^{-3}	Melting temp °C	Boiling temp °C	Abundance ppm
lithium	133	60	0.53	181	1330	65
sodium	157	95	0.97	98	890	28300
potassium	203	133	0.86	63	774	25900
rubidium	216	148	1.53	39	688	310
caesium	235	169	1.88	29	690	7

All of these properties come from the relatively weak metallic bonding; there is only one electron available per atom to be delocalised around the crystal, and the atoms themselves are the largest of their period. The crystal structure of the metals is body-centred cubic, a type of packing which does not bring the atoms as close together as the commoner hexagonal close-packed or face-centred cubic lattices can. Lithium is the least dense of all solid elements, and it and sodium and potassium float on water – as they react with it. As the atoms get larger, the bonding becomes weaker, so the melting temperatures and the hardness fall with increasing atomic number. The density rises, however, because the mass of the atom increases more rapidly than the size with increasing atomic number.

The first two ionisation energies and the reduction potentials for the alkali metals are given in Table 4.2, below.

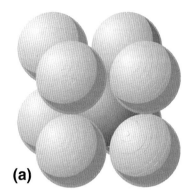

(a)

Table 4.2 *Ionisation energies and reduction potentials of Group 1 elements*

Element	First ionisation energy/kJ mol⁻¹	Second ionisation energy/kJ mol⁻¹	Standard reduction potential/V
lithium	520	7298	−3.03
sodium	496	4563	−2.71
potassium	419	3051	−2.92
rubidium	403	2632	−2.93
caesium	376	2420	−3.02

The alkali metals have one s electron outside a closed inert-gas configuration, from $1s^2 2s^1$ for lithium to $[Xe]6s^1$ for caesium. The first ionization energies decrease with increasing relative atomic mass. The nuclear charge increases on descending the group, but the increasing number of electron shells between the nucleus and the outermost electron shield the outer electron from the nuclear charge. An alternative view is that the inner electron shells repel the outer electron. Either way, the increase in shielding outweighs the increase in nuclear charge so that the effective nuclear charge, that is the actual charge which attracts the electron, falls, and so do the first ionization energies.

Second ionization energies are considerably larger than the first, since to remove the second electron would require breaking into the inert-gas structure. This penultimate shell is much closer to the nucleus (look at Table 4.1 to see the difference between the size of the atom and the size of the ion), the effective nuclear charge is much larger, and so the electrons are more strongly held.

The electrode potentials change in a similar way to the ionisation energies, with the notable exception of lithium. The relationship between ionisation energy and electrode potential has already been discussed in chapter 2; the perhaps surprising value of $E^{\ominus}$ for lithium, considering its relatively low reactivity in water, is due almost wholly to the large hydration enthalpy of the small Li^+ ion, with its high charge density.

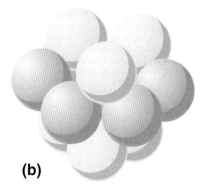

(b)

Figure 4.1(a) body-centred cubic arrangement of atoms; (b) hexagonal close-packed arrangement

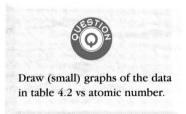

Draw (small) graphs of the data in table 4.2 vs atomic number.

Group 2

Various physical quantities concerning group 2, the alkaline earth metals, are given in Table 4.3 below.

Table 4.3. *Some physical quantities for Group 2 elements*

Element	Atomic radius/pm	Ionic radius/pm	Density g cm^{-3}	Melting temp °C	Boiling temp °C	Abundance ppm
beryllium	89	31	1.85	1278	2477	6
magnesium	136	65	1.74	649	1110	20900
calcium	174	97	1.54	839	1487	36300
strontium	191	113	2.6	769	1380	150
barium	198	135	3.51	725	1640	430

Draw (small) graphs of the data in table 4.3 vs atomic number.

The trends in atomic radius and ionization energy are the same on descending this group as they are for Group 1, and the explanations for this are similar. Densities are higher than Group 1 but still low for metals in general; this is partly because the atoms are smaller in Group 2, but also because the crystal structures are closely packed (apart from that of barium, which has body-centred cubic packing), and two electrons per atom are available for metallic bonding. Melting points are therefore higher than the corresponding metals in Group 1, and the metals are harder.

Table 4.4 lists the first three ionisation energies and the standard reduction potentials for the alkaline earth metals.

Table 4.4. *Ionisation energies and reduction potentials for Group 2 elements*

Element	First ionisation energy/kJ mol^{-1}	Second ionisation energy/kJ mol^{-1}	Third ionisation energy/kJ mol^{-1}	Reduction potential/V
beryllium	900	1757	14800	−1.85
magnesium	738	1451	7740	−2.37
calcium	590	1145	4940	−2.87
strontium	550	1064	4120	−2.89
barium	503	965	3390	−2.9

Draw (small) graphs of the data in table 4.4 vs atomic number.

The first and second ionisation energies are higher for Group 2 than for Group 1; the nuclear charge is greater, but the shielding of the outer electron by inner shells of electrons is similar. Thus, comparing sodium and magnesium, the outer electron in each case is in the $3s$ shell and they have the same inner electron configuration $1s^2\,2s^2\,2p^6$. The nuclear charge of magnesium is +12 compared to that of sodium which is +11, and the atom is smaller. Hence the attraction for the outer electrons in magnesium is larger so they are more difficult to remove. The large jump to the third ionisation energy is because this would involve breaking into closed shells.

The electrode potentials parallel the ionisation energies quite well; the value for beryllium would be expected to be more negative by analogy with lithium, but the difference is here due to the relatively large second ionisation energy of beryllium.

Some reactions of the *s*-block metals

The reactions of the *s*-block are fairly simple with few complicating features, so can be considered together. Beryllium excepted, the compounds are essentially ionic, and the only oxidation states shown are the group states, +1 and +2. In both cases this is because going above these entails an ionisation energy input which could not be recouped from the lattice enthalpy of the resulting solid. Similarly, $MgCl_2$ is formed rather than $MgCl$ because the increased lattice enthalpy more than compensates for the second ionisation energy of magnesium (see chapter 1, page 7).

Reactions of the *s*-block with oxygen

The reactions with oxygen highlight the only significant idiosyncrasies within the chemistry that concerns us, since the alkali metals do not all behave in the same way. All of the normal oxides are basic with the exception of beryllium oxide, which is amphoteric.

Lithium burns in oxygen with a deep red flame to form the usual oxide containing the O^{2-} ion:

$$4Li(s) \quad + \quad O_2(g) \quad \rightarrow \quad 2Li_2O(s)$$

Lithium oxide is a white solid.

Sodium burns in oxygen with a yellow flame to give a mixture of sodium oxide Na_2O, and sodium peroxide, Na_2O_2, the latter predominating in excess oxygen:

$$2Na(s) \quad + \quad O_2(g) \quad \rightarrow \quad Na_2O_2(s)$$

Sodium peroxide contains the peroxide ion, O_2^{2-}, in which the oxidation state of oxygen is (–1). Sodium peroxide is a pale yellow solid.

The remaining alkali metals form superoxides, which contain the O_2^- ion. This has an unpaired electron and is therefore a radical anion; one of the oxygen atoms does not have a full octet of electrons. Superoxides are exceptional among Group 1 compounds not containing transition metal ions in that they are coloured. KO_2 is yellow, RbO_2 orange, and CsO_2 red. Potassium, for example, burns with a lilac flame to give potassium superoxide, KO_2:

$$K(s) \quad + \quad O_2(g) \quad \rightarrow \quad KO_2(s)$$

All Group 1 metals will also react readily with the oxygen in the air at room temperature. Silvery when freshly cut, they rapidly tarnish and become dull due to a coating of oxide. For this reason, lithium, sodium and potassium are usually stored under paraffin oil, while rubidium and caesium which are much more reactive are stored in sealed containers. Lithium also reacts significantly with the nitrogen in the air, and forms a mixture of lithium oxide and lithium nitride, Li_3N.

GROUPS 1 AND 2

Give the equation representing the reaction of lithium with nitrogen. What ions are present in lithium nitride?

Give the equation for the reaction of magnesium with steam, and suggest why magnesium oxide is formed under such conditions rather than magnesium hydroxide.

Give the equations representing the reactions occurring when carbon dioxide is passed through limewater until there is no further change.

Except for barium, the elements of Group 2 all form their oxide on heating in oxygen. Magnesium burns with a brilliant white flame which is used for flares and in fireworks, calcium has a brick-red flame, and strontium deep red. These are the same as the colours which their compounds impart to the Bunsen flame and which are used in analysis (see below, p48). The equation representing the reaction of magnesium with oxygen is typical:

$$2Mg(s) \quad + \quad O_2(g) \quad \rightarrow \quad 2MgO(s)$$

The oxides are white solids, and are basic. Barium burns with an apple green flame to give a mixture of the oxide and white barium peroxide, Ba_2O_2.

In its reaction with oxygen, lithium behaves more like a Group 2 metal than a Group 1 metal. Lithium shows anomalies in other properties, and overall behaves in many ways like magnesium. This is an example of a diagonal relationship; another is that between beryllium and aluminium, which behave similarly. Beryllium oxide is amphoteric, for example, as is aluminium oxide.

Reactions of the *s*-block elements with water

All the *s*-block metals will react readily with cold water except for beryllium and magnesium. Beryllium is not attacked at all; magnesium reacts very slowly with cold water, but much more quickly with hot water or steam. The rate of reaction is generally faster for Group 1 than Group 2 and increases on descending each group. Hydrogen is liberated, and except for magnesium where magnesium oxide is formed, the hydroxide of the metal is produced. In the case of lithium, sodium and potassium, the metals float on the surface of the water, melt, and often burst into flame. The reaction of sodium with water is typical for Group 1:

$$2Na(s) \quad + \quad 2H_2O(l) \quad \rightarrow \quad 2NaOH(aq) \quad + \quad H_2(g)$$

The sodium rushes about on the surface of the water and the hydrogen often burns with a golden-yellow flame. Rubidium and caesium react explosively but the reaction is essentially the same.

The only significant difference for Group 2 metals is that the hydroxide formed is much less soluble and, in the case of calcium hydroxide, precipitates to give a milky-white suspension:

$$Ca(s) \quad + \quad 2H_2O(l) \quad \rightarrow \quad Ca(OH)_2(s) \quad + \quad H_2(g)$$

Reactions of the *s*-block elements with chlorine

All *s*-block elements react directly on heating with chlorine gas to form the chloride. The chlorides are ionic except for that of beryllium, which is covalent. It forms a polymer based on a linear molecule:

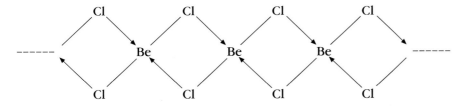

Figure 4.2 The linear molecule of beryllium chloride

The reactions of sodium and magnesium with chlorine are typical:

$$2Na(s) \ + \ Cl_2(g) \ \rightarrow \ 2\,NaCl(s)$$

$$Mg(s) \ + \ Cl_2(g) \ \rightarrow \ MgCl_2(s)$$

The ionic chlorides are all soluble in water. Magnesium chloride has some covalent character, as shown by the difference between the Born–Haber cycle value for the lattice enthalpy and the calculated value (chapter 1, page 8). If hydrated magnesium chloride is heated, some hydrolysis occurs and hydrogen chloride is evolved:

$$MgCl_2 \ + \ H_2O \ \rightleftharpoons \ Mg(OH)Cl \ + \ HCl$$

Hydrated magnesium chloride can be converted to the anhydrous salt by heating in a stream of hydrogen chloride gas. Why?

Reactions of the *s*-block oxides with water

All of the oxygen compounds mentioned earlier react with water. The oxides, containing O^{2-} ions, react to form the metal hydroxide:

$$O^{2-}(s) \ + \ H_2O(l) \ \rightarrow \ 2OH^-(aq)$$

Peroxides, containing the O_2^{2-} ion, react with water liberating hydrogen peroxide, H_2O_2:

$$O_2^{2-} \ + \ 2H_2O(l) \ \rightarrow \ 2OH^-(aq) \ + \ H_2O_2(aq)$$

Superoxides, with the O_2^- ion, react to form hydrogen peroxide and oxygen

$$2O_2^- \ + \ 2H_2O(l) \ \rightarrow \ 2OH^-(aq) \ + \ H_2O_2(aq) \ + \ O_2(g)$$

Thus all the solutions will be alkaline owing to the formation of the OH^- ion in solution. The reactions are of the anion, so they are independent of the cation present and are the same for Groups 1 and 2.

The solubilities of the hydroxides and sulphates of Group 2

The solubilities of the hydroxides and sulphates of Group 2 are summarised in table 4.5. The explanation for these trends is given in chapter 1, page 9.

Table 4.5. *Solubilities of Group 2 sulphates and hydroxides*

Ion	ΔH_{hyd} (M^{2+}) /kJ mol^{-1}	Cation radius /pm	Sulphate solubility mol per 100g water	Hydroxide solubility mol per 100g water
Mg^{2+}	−1920	65	1.83×10^{-1}	2.00×10^{-5}
Ca^{2+}	−1650	99	4.66×10^{-3}	1.53×10^{-3}
Sr^{2+}	−1480	113	7.11×10^{-5}	3.37×10^{-3}
Ba^{2+}	−1360	135	9.43×10^{-7}	1.50×10^{-2}

The thermal stabilities of the carbonates and nitrates of Group 2

This material has been explained in chapter 1, page 11. The reactions are summarised here.

The carbonates of Group 2 decompose on heating; the decomposition of calcium carbonate is typical:

$$CaCO_3(s) \quad \rightarrow \quad CaO(s) \quad + \quad CO_2(g)$$

This reaction is important in cement manufacture and in the extraction of iron (chapter 6, page 72).

The thermal stabilities of Group 2 carbonates decrease in the order

$$BaCO_3 \quad >> \quad SrCO_3 \quad > \quad CaCO_3 \quad > \quad MgCO_3 \quad >> \quad BeCO_3$$

Barium carbonate does not decompose at Bunsen temperatures; all other group 2 carbonates decompose similarly to calcium carbonate, according to the equation above. Beryllium carbonate decomposes at room temperature.

Group 1 carbonates do not decompose at normal Bunsen temperatures. The exception is lithium carbonate, which decomposes to the oxide on heating:

$$Li_2CO_3(s) \quad \rightarrow \quad Li_2O(s) \quad + \quad CO_2(g).$$

Group 2 nitrates on heating all decompose to the metal oxide, brown nitrogen dioxide, and oxygen. Calcium nitrate is typical:

$$2Ca(NO_3)_2(s) \quad \rightarrow \quad 2CaO(s) \quad + \quad 4NO_2(g) \ + \ O_2(g)$$

In the case of Group 1 nitrates, the thermal decomposition product is the nitrite. Sodium nitrate is typical:

$$2NaNO_3(s) \quad \rightarrow \quad 2NaNO_2(s) \quad + \quad O_2(g)$$

No brown gas is evolved. The nitrates are all white and the nitrites pale yellow.

The sources of *s*-block elements

The commonest *s*-block elements are sodium, potassium, magnesium and calcium. All of the elements are far too reactive to occur native, that is as the uncombined metal.

Sodium chloride, as rock salt, is found in enormous deposits all over the world, in the UK principally in Cheshire. It is mined conventionally, but also by solution mining. In this technique water is pumped into underlying salt strata and the resulting brine then used. Unless done carefully, solution mining can lead to substantial and unpredictable subsidence, a feature of the Cheshire landscape. A section of the Trent and Mersey canal outside Middlewich had to be embanked by tens of feet in a matter of weeks in the 19th century owing to subsidence. Sodium chloride is also found in seawater, of course, but at rather low concentration, so this only serves as a source of sodium chloride crystals in hot countries where the crystals are found naturally at the edge of the water. Sodium nitrate is found in substantial deposits in Chile, but was at one time of more interest for the nitrate content, originally used to make nitric acid, than for its sodium.

Potassium is obtained principally from the soluble mineral carnallite, $KCl.MgCl_2.6H_2O$, at Stassfurt. Lithium, rubidium and caesium are found mainly in rather rare, insoluble aluminosilicate minerals.

Magnesium is present in seawater as well as in carnallite. Another major source is dolomite, an insoluble double carbonate of calcium and magnesium, $MgCO_3.CaCO_3$. Calcium is very widely distributed as insoluble calcium carbonate in the form of limestone, marble and chalk, and also as the insoluble sulphate in gypsum, $CaSO_4.2H_2O$. Strontium and barium are found as their insoluble sulphates; beryllium is found in beryl, a pale green insoluble aluminosilicate which is used as a semi-precious stone.

All of the metals are extracted from their chlorides, so conversion to these is necessary for the extraction of metals other than sodium or potassium. The electrolysis of sodium chloride in various forms, the basis of the chlor–alkali industry, is covered in the next chapter.

Flame colours and their analytical uses

Some of the s-block metals or their compounds impart a characteristic colour to a Bunsen flame: Table 4.6.

Table 4.6. *Flame colours of the s–block elements*

Group 1	lithium	carmine red
	sodium	yellow
	potassium	lilac
Group 2	calcium	brick red
	strontium	crimson red
	barium	apple green

The flame test can be used to identify the presence of these elements; the reds are difficult to describe, and in the case of Li and Sr difficult to tell apart. The flame test is performed by picking up a speck of the test compound on a platinum wire which has been moistened with concentrated hydrochloric acid (the chlorides being the most volatile compounds), then placing the sample at the edge of a roaring bunsen flame (see Figure 4.3). The heat energy of the flame causes electrons to be excited within the metal atoms. When these return to lower energy levels they emit light of characteristic frequencies and therefore colour. This can be observed qualitatively, or can be analysed in a (visible) spectrometer. This shows a spectrum which consists of a series of lines of definite frequency, each line corresponding to a particular electron transition, and not equally distributed throughout the spectrum. The series of lines produced is a line spectrum and is unique to a particular element. The spectrum for sodium is shown in Figure 4.4. Alkali metals and alkaline earth metals have strong lines in the visible region of the spectrum. Sticks of sodium chloride were at one time sold to enable the production of sodium light in the laboratory, for example for the investigation of optical activity. Sodium light is virtually monochromatic.

Flame spectra can also be used quantitatively; the flame photometer can measure the concentrations of sodium and potassium in body fluids, for example. In astronomy, the spectra can be used to analyse the atmosphere of other planets. Helium was found on the sun, via the absorption spectrum of sunlight, before it was found on Earth.

Figure 4.3 The flame colours of (left to right): sodium, potassium, calcium, strontium, barium and lithium

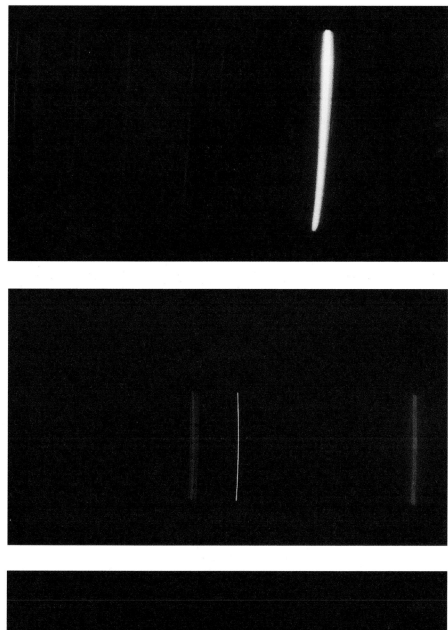

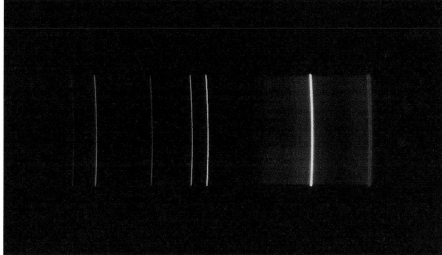

Figure 4.4 The spectrum of sodium, top, (an alkali metal) compared with those of hydrogen, centre, and helium

The chlor–alkali industry

The chlor–alkali industry, so-called because it involves the simultaneous production of chlorine and sodium hydroxide, is one of the most significant of heavy chemical industries. There would be very little other manufacturing industry, and a serious public health problem, in the absence of its products.

Electrolysis is used to manufacture chlorine and sodium hydroxide.
The chlor-alkali industry is the second largest consumer of electricity in the chemical industry, the aluminium industry being the largest.

Since this is the first place in the London scheme where electrolysis appears, the necessary principles will be revised before addressing the manufacturing processes themselves.

Electrolysis

Electrolysis
The chemical breakdown of a substance (electrolyte) in solution or when molten, caused by the passage of an electric current

Electrolysis ('breaking by electricity') is the passage of an electric current accompanied by chemical change. The compound to be electrolysed must be ionic. The charge carriers are ions, which must be free to move, so the compound must be molten (or fused), or in solution. Often, but not necessarily, this is a solution in water. In some cases solutions in molten salts are used; the electrolyte for the production of aluminium (chapter 6, page 69) is a solution of aluminium oxide in molten sodium aluminium fluoride. The melt or the solution is called the electrolyte.

The current from the power source, which is an electron flow, is introduced into the electrolyte by electrodes, often made from graphite, sometimes metal. The main requirement is that the products at the electrodes should not react with the electrode material, though in aluminium production even this concern is ignored (see page 69). The power source produces an excess of electrons at one electrode which becomes negatively charged; the cathode. Electrons are withdrawn from the other electrode which becomes positively charged; the anode. The rate at which materials are produced at the electrodes depends on the rate at which electrons are transferred, that is on the current. In industry very heavy currents of the order of 30 000A are used.

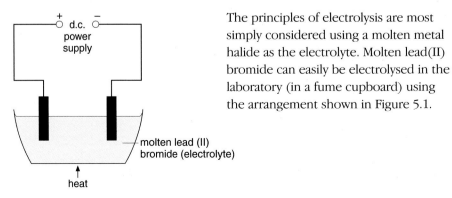

The principles of electrolysis are most simply considered using a molten metal halide as the electrolyte. Molten lead(II) bromide can easily be electrolysed in the laboratory (in a fume cupboard) using the arrangement shown in Figure 5.1.

Figure 5.1 Electrolysis of molten lead(II) bromide

When current is supplied, the positive ions Pb^{2+} move in the electric field set up between the electrodes towards the negative electrode, the cathode. Positive ions are therefore cations. The negative ions Br^- move to the positive electrode, the anode, and are anions. If the applied voltage is large enough, the ions will undergo oxidation or reduction and will be discharged.

At the cathode, electrons are available and will be acquired by the cations; electron gain is reduction. At **C**athodes redu**C**tion occurs. The lead(II) ions form lead metal which, since it has a lower melting temperature ($327\,°C$) than the lead (II) bromide electrolyte ($373\,°C$), collects as a pool on the bottom of the vessel.

Cathode
At **C**athodes redu**C**tion occurs

$$Pb^{2+} \quad + \quad 2e^- \quad \rightarrow \quad Pb$$

At the same time Br^- ions give up their electrons to the electron-deficient anode, and are oxidised. At **A**nodes oxid**A**tion occurs. Bromine gas is liberated:

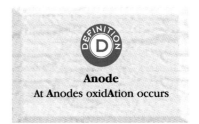

Anode
At **A**nodes oxid**A**tion occurs

$$Br^- \quad \rightarrow \quad \tfrac{1}{2}Br_2 \quad + \quad e^-$$

Lead(II) bromide has been decomposed into the elements lead and bromine. The overall equation for the decomposition is obtained by adding the half-equations after making the number of electrons in each the same:

$$Pb^{2+} \quad + \quad 2e^- \quad \rightarrow \quad Pb$$

$$2Br^- \quad \rightarrow \quad Br_2 \quad + \quad 2e^-$$

Overall: $\quad Pb^{2+} \quad + \quad 2Br^- \quad \rightarrow \quad Pb \quad + \quad Br_2$

Ionic movement is necessary for electrolysis – the word ion is Greek meaning 'going' or 'wanderer'. Compounds where both ions are coloured, such as copper(II) chromate(VI), $CuCrO_4$, can be used to show the movement of ions in an electric field. If green copper(II) chromate(VI) solution is placed in the middle of a piece of wet filter paper and a potential difference applied via crocodile clips, the blue $Cu^{2+}(aq)$ ion will move towards the cathode and the yellow $CrO_4^{2-}(aq)$ ion towards the anode. The separation can be seen clearly after a short time.

Electrolysis of mixed electrolytes

In the discussion above concerning lead(II) bromide, we saw that the ions discharge if the voltage 'is large enough'. This statement requires a little elaboration, since the electrolytes we are mainly interested in contain mixtures, with several cations and several anions. You need to have an idea of why the products are as they are, although the detailed reasons related to the electrode potentials are not at present examinable in the London scheme.

The electrolyte used in the chlor–alkali industry is concentrated aqueous sodium chloride, brine. It must be concentrated; seawater will not do, which is a pity given its availability. Brine contains two cations, $Na^+(aq)$ from the salt and $H^+(aq)$ from the ionisation of the water solvent; and two anions, $Cl^-(aq)$ and $OH^-(aq)$ from the same sources. Electrolysis of brine gives hydrogen from the reduction of $H^+(aq)$ at the cathode; sodium ions are not discharged. It is often said that the hydrogen ions are preferentially discharged. At the anode, chloride ions are preferentially discharged over hydroxide ions in concentrated solutions, but the position is reversed in dilute solutions, which is why seawater is of no use. Electrolysis of seawater gives oxygen at the anode.

The reasons are related to the electrochemical series, that is to the standard electrode potentials. In an electrochemical cell, a potential is produced from chemical processes at the electrodes; if the potential is matched from an external source, there will be no chemical changes, and if the potential is exceeded, then the chemical processes may be reversed. This is the basis for the recharging of the lead–acid cell, described in chapter 2, p32. To discharge ions in a cell, an electrical potential approximately equal to or larger than the standard cell potential must be applied.

The potential is not exactly predictable, even though the standard cell potential will be known. There are several reasons for this:

- the solutions used in electrolysis are not usually at 1.00 mol dm^{-3} concentration, so the conditions are not standard conditions. The order in which ions discharge can change markedly with changes in concentration;

- the actual value of the discharge potential is not precisely defined even for standard solutions;

- the discharge potential depends on the surface condition of the electrode, so it is not the same for polished electrodes as it is for roughened ones;

- the discharge potential depends on the material from which the electrodes are made, and may differ widely from the standard potential for the particular cell in question.

This is particularly striking in the case of a cell which uses a mercury cathode with a brine electrolyte; sodium ions are preferentially discharged over hydrogen ions under these conditions, and the sodium forms an alloy, or amalgam, with the mercury. This mercury cathode or Castner–Kellner–Solvay cell is still widely (though decreasingly) used as a manufacturing method for sodium hydroxide. The sodium amalgam produced is pumped away and reacted with water in presence of a graphite catalyst. The mercury is returned to the electrolysis cell.

Despite all these comments, it is usually the case that ions will be discharged from a mixed electrolyte in the same order as they appear in the electrochemical series. Thus copper(II) ions ($E^\ominus = +0.34V$) will be discharged in preference to $H^+(aq)$ ($E^\ominus = 0.00V$), followed by Zn^{2+} ($E^\ominus = -0.76$ V), and so on. The more negative the metal ion's reduction potential, the larger the voltage needed to discharge it. Anions become more difficult to discharge the more positive their reduction potential becomes; thus iodide ions ($E^\ominus = +0.54V$) will be discharged preferentially to chloride ions ($E^\ominus = +1.36V$).

The effect of concentration on the discharge of anions can be seen in the electrolysis of an aqueous solution of sodium chloride. The anions present are $Cl^-(aq)$ and $OH^-(aq)$. At the anode, oxygen is liberated by oxidation of hydroxide ions if the solution is dilute:

$$4OH^-(aq) \rightarrow O_2(g) + 2H_2O(l) + 4e^-$$

At the cathode, hydrogen ions are discharged, so the overall cell reaction is:

$$2H_2O \rightarrow 2H_2(g) + O_2(g)$$

The result is that the water is electrolysed. The presence of small concentrations of sodium chloride has no effect on the ions discharged, but it does increase the conductivity of the electrolyte considerably so that electrolysis is much faster than it would be with water alone.

If the sodium chloride solution is more concentrated, greater than 23% or so, chlorine is liberated from the anode:

$$2Cl^- \rightarrow Cl_2 + 2e^-$$

so the overall cell reaction is:

$$2NaCl(aq) + 2H_2O(l) \rightarrow H_2(g) + Cl_2(g) + 2NaOH(aq).$$

It is this reaction that is the basis of the chlor–alkali industry.

The manufacture of sodium

Sodium is made by the electrolysis of molten sodium chloride. The high melting temperature of sodium chloride (801°C) requires the addition of calcium chloride to bring the electrolyte melting temperature down and reduce the energy needed to keep it molten.

The electrolyte is contained in the Downs Cell, a cell which is made of ceramic-lined steel with the electrolyte at a temperature of about 600°C. A number of graphite anodes are surrounded by an iron gauze diaphragm and a steel cathode. A diagram of such a cell is shown in Figure 5.2.

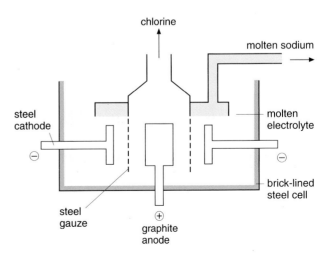

Figure 5.2 A Downs cell

Sodium ions migrate to the steel cathodes and are discharged:

$$Na^+ + e^- \rightarrow Na$$

The sodium metal is liquid at the temperature of the cell, and being less dense than the electrolyte floats on it. It is removed from the cell through a cooled tube.

Chlorine gas is liberated at the graphite anodes:

$$2Cl^- \rightarrow Cl_2 + 2e^-$$

Chlorine is thus a useful coproduct.

Cells will last between one and two years under the conditions used, typically $25 - 40 \times 10^3 A$ at about 7V. The cell life is determined by loss of graphite from the anodes. This can occur because if any oxides are present in the electrolyte oxide ions will discharge at the anode giving oxygen. This erodes the graphite anode by forming carbon monoxide or carbon dioxide. The steel gauze diaphragm keeps the anode and cathode compartments separate so that the chlorine does not react with the sodium, converting it back to sodium chloride. The diaphragm requires replacement at approximately fortnightly intervals since the steel is attacked by chlorine.

The main impurity in the sodium produced is calcium, which is also discharged in small amount at the cathode. Up to 5% calcium might be present initially but some of this precipitates out as the molten sodium is cooled. Any remaining calcium is removed by filtration at around 110°C, reducing the calcium impurity to about 0.04%.

The manufacture of sodium hydroxide

Sodium hydroxide is manufactured together with chlorine by the electrolysis of sodium chloride solution. We have already considered the electrochemistry, so we shall now look at the technology.

The Gibbs diaphragm cell

The essential requirement for the industrial implementation of this process is an economic and effective method for separation of the reactions occurring at the anode and the cathode. In one type of diaphragm cell, this is achieved by using a porous diaphragm, usually of asbestos, between the anode and cathode compartments. This allows the flow of brine from anode to cathode but separates the chlorine and hydrogen gas and prevents the reaction of chlorine with the sodium hydroxide solution in the cathode compartment. Also, because of the velocity of the liquid flow from one compartment to the other, back migration of hydroxide ions from the cathode to the anode is reduced. A diagrammatic representation of the Gibbs Diaphragm cell is shown in Figure 5.3. The anodes are of titanium, and the cathodes of steel

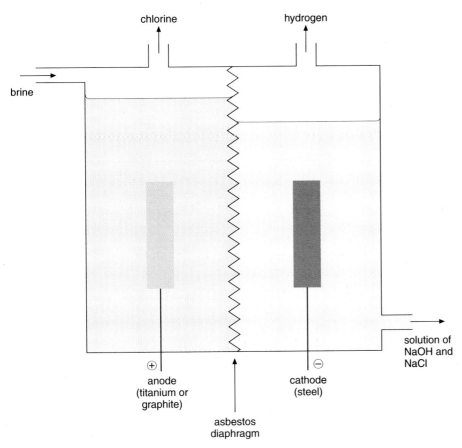

Figure 5.3 The diaphragm cell

As the hydrogen ions are discharged, hydroxide ions accumulate in the cathode compartment together with aqueous sodium ions, to produce a solution of sodium hydroxide. The hydrogen gas and chlorine gas are pumped away, and used to make hydrogen chloride for conversion to hydrochloric acid. The electrolyte is kept at a higher level in the anode compartment so that the used brine percolates through the diaphragm into the cathode compartment, where it is removed along with the sodium hydroxide solution.

The cathode solution might contain typically 10% sodium hydroxide and 15% sodium chloride by mass. The volume of this solution is reduced by evaporation; the much less soluble sodium chloride crystallises out on cooling to leave a solution containing about 50% sodium hydroxide by mass with less than 1% sodium chloride.

The brine fed to the Gibbs cell has to be freed from magnesium and calcium ions. If this is not done, the diaphragm is blocked by precipitates of magnesium or calcium hydroxide.

A more recent version of the Gibbs cell uses an ion-exchange membrane rather than the asbestos diaphragm. This gives a purer product, but the cells are expensive to set up and maintain. Nevertheless they will gradually replace the Gibbs and Castner–Kellner–Solvay cells.

The manufacture of sodium chlorate(I)

Sodium chlorate(I), NaOCl, more commonly known as sodium hypochlorite, is used in large quantities as bleach. It is the principal ingredient in domestic bleach, for example. It is made by allowing the chlorine and the sodium hydroxide from the Gibbs cell to mix at room temperature. The chlorine is simultaneously oxidised and reduced, so the reaction is a disproportionation reaction (chapter 7, page 78). The oxidation states of the chlorine are shown under the ionic equation:

$$Cl_2(g) + 2OH^-(aq) \rightarrow OCl^-(aq) + Cl^-(aq) + H_2O(l)$$
$$(0) \qquad\qquad\qquad (+1) \qquad (-1)$$

The full equation is:

$$Cl_2(g) + 2NaOH(aq) \rightarrow NaOCl(aq) + NaCl(aq) + H_2O(l)$$

For most purposes the presence of sodium chloride in the bleach does not matter, and all domestic bleach contains it. However, in acid solution sodium chlorate(I) is an oxidising agent and will oxidise chloride ions to chlorine:

$$OCl^-(aq) + 2H^+(aq) + Cl^-(aq) \rightarrow Cl_2(g) + H_2O(l)$$

This is why domestic bleach carries the warning that it must not be mixed with other materials, in case chlorine is liberated. Some other cleaning materials, for example, contain sodium hydrogen sulphate, which is acidic.

The uses of the products from the chlor–alkali industry

The London scheme requires that the uses of the materials dealt with above are known. A little more detail is given here so that these uses can be put into their proper background, but this detail is not examinable unless specifically required by other sections of the syllabus. Such uses are cross-referenced. 'Use' implies large-scale industrial use unless stated to the contrary. Most of these substances have a wide range of uses, and only the more significant are mentioned here.

Sodium

Coolant in nuclear reactors: sodium is used as a heat-transfer medium for nuclear reactors, to conduct the heat from the core and transfer it to steam-generating plant. This is because, in spite of the handling problems associated with molten sodium, it has a high thermal capacity (1.23 kJ kg^{-1} K^{-1}, some 23% higher than water) and is therefore very efficient.

Wire: provided sodium is coated with an insulator to keep air out in addition to its electrical function, sodium wires are very flexible and have been used in some specialised applications.

Street lighting: the familiar yellow street lamps pass a current through sodium vapour. Electrons in the atoms are excited to higher energy levels by collision with current electrons; when they fall back to lower energy levels light is emitted. Sodium light is nearly monochromatic, and is often used in the laboratory where a simple source of such light is needed. In less complex times, sticks of sodium chloride were sold for this purpose, and were clamped in a Bunsen flame - a slightly different use for the flame test.

Some street lamps employ sodium vapour at high pressure and have a fluorescent material lining the glass; their light is not monochromatic.

As a reducing agent: sodium is used as a reducing agent in the manufacture of tetraethyllead, $Pb(C_2H_5)_4$. This is a declining use with the decreasing consumption of leaded petrol (see Module 4, topic 23). Sodium in ethanol can also be used in the laboratory to reduce organic compounds, for example aldehydes or ketones to alcohols.

Production of salts: some sodium salts are made from sodium metal. Chief amongst these is sodium cyanide, NaCN, used in the extraction of gold, silver and other precious metals. Molten sodium is reacted with ammonia at 300–400°C, and the product from this treated with red-hot charcoal:

$$2Na \; + \; 2NH_3 \; \rightarrow \; 2NaNH_2 \; + \; H_2$$

$$2NaNH_2 \; + \; 2C \; \rightarrow \; 2NaCN \; + \; 2H_2.$$

Manufacture of titanium: titanium is made by the reduction of titanium(IV) chloride with magnesium ar sodium in an atmosphere of argon:

$$TiCl_4 \; + \; 4Na \; \rightarrow \; Ti \; + \; 4NaCl$$

Titanium is important in aircraft manufacture.

Figure 5.4 Sodium vapour used in street lighting

Sodium hydroxide

Soap making (see also Module 2 Chapter 8).

The manufacture of modern types of soap, made by the alkaline hydrolysis of various sorts of fat, began in Italy in the 8th century. Originally goat fat was used. Hard soaps are made by boiling the fat with sodium hydroxide solution. Animal fat, fish oil, or various sorts of vegetable oil such as coconut, olive, palm, soybean or corn are used. The soap produced is the sodium salt of a long-chain carboxylic acid, and the important coproduct is propan–1,2,3-triol or glycerol. This finds use in pharmaceuticals, cosmetics, lubricants and antifreeze.

Figure 5.5 A battery of cells for the electrolysis of brine at Hays Chemicals, Cheshire

The essential reaction is illustrated by the hydrolysis of tristearin, found in beef fat:

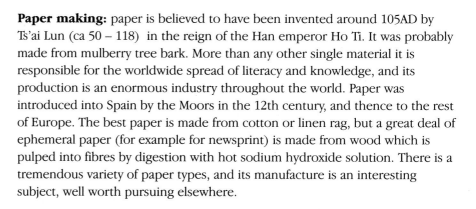

$$C_{17}H_{35}COOCH_2$$
|
$$C_{17}H_{35}COOCH \quad + \quad 3NaOH \quad \rightarrow \quad 3C_{17}H_{35}COO^-Na^+ \quad + \quad$$
|
$$C_{17}H_{35}COOCH_2$$

$$HOCH_2$$
|
$$HOCH$$
|
$$HOCH_2$$

tristearin   sodium stearate   glycerol
                               [soap]

The subtleties of soap varieties are beyond our present concerns, but it is perhaps interesting that coconut oil, which unlike most other vegetable oils is almost wholly a saturated fat (in fact much more saturated than butterfat), produces a soap that lathers very poorly in fresh water. In seawater it works perfectly well, so coconut oil is used to produce marine soap.

The reaction of sodium hydroxide with fats is the reason it is used as a degreasing agent; it also makes it one of the most dangerous materials in common use to get into the eye. *Any* contact between eyes and sodium hydroxide *must* always receive medical attention, however trivial the event might seem at the time.

Paper making: paper is believed to have been invented around 105AD by Ts'ai Lun (ca 50 – 118) in the reign of the Han emperor Ho Ti. It was probably made from mulberry tree bark. More than any other single material it is responsible for the worldwide spread of literacy and knowledge, and its production is an enormous industry throughout the world. Paper was introduced into Spain by the Moors in the 12th century, and thence to the rest of Europe. The best paper is made from cotton or linen rag, but a great deal of ephemeral paper (for example for newsprint) is made from wood which is pulped into fibres by digestion with hot sodium hydroxide solution. There is a tremendous variety of paper types, and its manufacture is an interesting subject, well worth pursuing elsewhere.

Rayon manufacture: rayon is a synthetic fibre made from cellulose. The cellulose is first converted to a sticky liquid intermediate, viscose. This is extruded through fine holes into an acid bath to form the hardened fibres which can then be spun into yarn. There are two varieties of viscose; one is made by the treatment of cellulose with sodium hydroxide solution, followed by carbon disulphide CS_2. The other uses an ammoniacal solution of tetramminecopper(II) ions, $[Cu(NH_3)_4]^{2+}$ (see 'complex ions' in Module 1). which will dissolve cellulose; treatment of the resulting solution with sodium hydroxide solution gives the other variety of viscose.

Figure 5.6 Paper making.
A technician loads wood chips into the hopper of a pulping plant (top); finished paper is rolled to smooth it out (bottom)

Aluminium extraction: large amounts of sodium hydroxide are used in the purification of bauxite prior to its electrolysis in the Hall–Heroult cell for aluminium production. This is dealt with in detail in chapter 6, pages 69-70.

Sodium hydroxide also finds wide use as a general purpose alkali, for example in making other salts.

Chlorine

Water treatment: huge quantities of chlorine are used to sterilise water for drinking. This use, together with the efficient sewage handling introduced in the 19th century, has been one of the most important factors leading to the elimination of cholera and typhoid in many parts of the world, including the UK. Cholera was endemic in London as recently as the 19th century.

Some chlorine is also used for sewage treatment.

Organochlorine manufacture: chlorine reacts with many organic compounds to produce useful materials. With methane, for example, it gives tetrachloromethane CCl_4, a solvent; and in other reactions gives useful pesticides. The use of organochlorine compounds is in decline, partly because of problems such as toxicity and ozone-layer depletion from chlorofluorocarbons, so much work is currently in progress to find alternatives. (See chapter 7, pages 81-83).

Hydrochloric acid manufacture: hydrochloric acid is one of the cheapest acids, and is widely used as a general purpose strong acid where strong oxidising agents (which would give chlorine) are absent. Made from combustion of hydrogen in chlorine, it is in turn used to make metal chlorides, to clean the surface of metals prior to electroplating, and (perhaps somewhat surprisingly) to make corn syrup and glucose from corn starch.

PVC manufacture: large amounts of chlorine are used to make polyvinyl chloride, PVC. This is described in chapter 7, page 82.

Bromine manufacture: bromine is extracted by oxidation with chlorine of the bromide ions present in seawater (chapter 7, page 74):

$$2Br^-(aq) \quad + \quad Cl_2(aq) \quad \rightarrow \quad Br_2(aq) \quad + \quad 2Cl^-(aq)$$

Hydrogen

Hydrochloric acid manufacture: this has been mentioned above in connection with chlorine.

Hydrogen is also used for the following purposes. However, the hydrogen from the chlor–alkali industry is virtually entirely used for hydrochloric acid manufacture, and does not find its way to these other uses.

Ammonia manufacture: hydrogen is reacted with nitrogen in the Haber process for the production of ammonia, in turn used for the manufacture of fertilizers, nitric acid and explosives. The reaction, which is represented by

$$N_2(g) \quad + \quad 3H_2(g) \quad \rightleftharpoons \quad 2NH_3(g),$$

is discussed in Module 2 Chapter 3, Chemical equilibrium.

Margarine manufacture: margarine was invented by Hippolyte Mège-Mouriès in 1869 as a butter substitute. Oils, which can be of animal or vegetable origin, are reacted with hydrogen at 200°C and 3–4 atm pressure in presence of a nickel catalyst. A number of the carbon–carbon double bonds found in the oils are saturated, and the products are solid:

Soya bean or cottonseed oil is widely used; fish oils are also hydrogenated for eventual conversion into soaps.

Rocket fuel: liquid hydrogen is used together with liquid oxygen as a rocket fuel.

Sodium chlorate(I)
Bleach: domestic bleach consists of sodium chlorate(I) (hypochlorite) and sodium chloride solution. It acts by oxidising coloured materials to colourless products.

Disinfectant: bleach has similar germicidal properties to chlorine, but being a liquid is much more convenient to handle.

Figure 5.7 Liquid hydrogen is a vital component of rocket fuel

Groups 3 and 4

We have already considered the chemistry of group 4 in Chapter 5 of Module 1 (The Periodic Table), where a number of chemical facts were presented. This chapter seeks to explain some of those facts, and to introduce comparisons with the chemistry of Group 3.

The increase in metallic character in Group 4

The chemistry of the elements in Group 4 changes from that of a non-metal in carbon to that of a metal in lead. Metallic character is considered to involve

- the formation of positive ions;

- the formation of predominantly ionic chlorides which do not hydrolyse significantly when placed in water;

- the formation of ionic oxides which are basic or amphoteric.

Carbon as a non-metal

Carbon forms covalent bonds; the isolated C^{4+} ion does not exist. This can be explained in two ways: C^{4+} would have an estimated ionic radius of 15 pm. Such a tiny, highly charged ion would be enormously polarising and would form covalent bonds. Alternatively: ionic compounds are favoured if the ionisation energies of the cation (endothermic) and the electron affinities of the anion (which overall may be exo– or endothermic) are compensated by the exothermic lattice enthalpy of the resulting compound. The first four ionisation energies of carbon are in total 14 270 kJ mol^{-1}, and there is no chance of recouping this through the lattice energy of any conceivable ionic solid.

Tetrachloromethane CCl_4 is liquid at room temperature, and is molecular covalent. It does not hydrolyse with water, unlike many covalent chlorides, but this is a kinetic effect which is explained below.

Carbon dioxide is acidic; it is a typical non-metal oxide.

Lead as a metal

Lead is really a semi-metal, showing characteristics both of metal and non-metal in its chemistry. The metallic nature predominates, however, and physical properties (density, conductivity, lustre) are metallic.

As the size of the atoms in the group increases, the ionisation energies fall. With lead (+2) the first two ionisation energies are sufficiently low to result in $PbCl_2$ being ionic and not hydrolysed by water. PbO and PbO_2 are both amphoteric; PbO_2 in addition is strongly oxidising.

Similar trends are seen in the chemistry of Group 3, though the semi-metallic nature appears sooner, at aluminum.

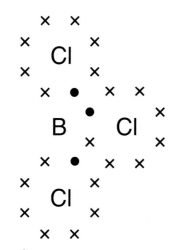

Figure 6.1

Some chlorides of Groups 3 and 4

Group 3

Boron is the only non-metal with fewer than 4 valence electrons: $1s^2 2s^2 2p^1$. This gives it electron-acceptor properties which dominate the chemistry of its chloride (and oxide). Aluminium chloride is similar in this respect.

Boron trichloride accepts electron pairs readily since the boron atom has only 6 electrons in its outer shell. Thus ammonia, which is an electron-pair donor, reacts with boron trichloride to form

$$H_3N: BCl_3 \qquad \text{or} \qquad H_3N \rightarrow BCl_3$$

Unlike aluminium chloride which dimerises to form Al_2Cl_6, boron trichloride remains as a monomer, and has the low boiling temperature of 13°C. The B–Cl bond is short enough to allow some of the electron density of the lone-pair electrons of the chlorine atoms to be 'back donated' into the empty p orbital on boron.

Boron trichloride is rapidly attacked by water, the water's lone pairs being readily accepted by the boron atom. The energy barrier to hydrolysis is therefore low:

$$BCl_3(g) \quad + \quad 3H_2O(l) \quad \rightarrow \quad B(OH)_3(aq) \quad + \quad 3HCl(aq)$$

The product is boric acid, which is written as $B(OH)_3$ rather than H_3BO_3 since it is not a triprotic (tribasic) acid.

Anhydrous aluminium chloride is dimeric (Al_2Cl_6), the Al–Cl bond being too long to allow back donation of electron density. Aluminium has an octet in the dimer.

State, and justify in terms of VSEPR theory, the shapes of Al_2Cl_6 and BCl_3.

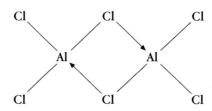

Figure 6.2 The dimer of aluminium chloride

Aluminium chloride hydrolyses in water, but the reaction is slower than with boron trichloride and does not go to completion. Aluminium hydroxide is not produced unless alkali is used. In the stepwise hydrolysis shown below the equilibrium of the third reaction lies well to the left:

$$AlCl_3(aq) + H_2O(l) \rightleftharpoons Al(OH)Cl_2(aq) + HCl(aq)$$

$$Al(OH)Cl_2(aq) + H_2O(l) \rightleftharpoons Al(OH)_2Cl(aq) + HCl(aq)$$

$$Al(OH)_2Cl(aq) + H_2O(l) \rightleftharpoons Al(OH)_3(s) + HCl(aq) .$$

The solution in water is therefore acidic but aluminium hydroxide is not precipitated.

The electron acceptor property of aluminium chloride is the reason for its use as a catalyst in the Friedel–Crafts reaction between an alkyl or acyl halide and an arene. It generates the electrophile by accepting electrons from the halogen atom of the alkyl or acyl halide. An example of this reaction is shown by the action of chloromethane on benzene:

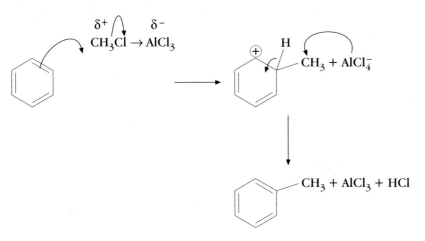

Figure 6.3 The action of chloromethane on benzene

This reaction is considered further in topic 23 of Module 4.

Group 4

Tetrachloromethane CCl_4 and silicon tetrachloride $SiCl_4$ show marked differences from one another and from the Group 3 halides. Both are molecular covalent; the bonds are polar, but the tetrahedral shape of the molecule means that the dipoles cancel and the molecules have no overall dipole moment.

Write a series of equations to represent the deprotonation by hydroxide ions of $[Al(H_2O)_6]^{3+}$ to produce $Al(OH)_3(H_2O)_3$.

Write mechanisms representing the reactions between the following substances in the presence of aluminium chloride:
(a) benzene and ethanoyl chloride CH_3COCl;
(b) benzene and 2-chloro-2-methylpropane.

Tetrachloromethane is not attacked by water at room temperature; the liquids are immiscible. Even at 1000°C it hydrolyses only partially:

$$CCl_4 \quad + \quad H_2O \quad \rightarrow \quad COCl_2 \quad + \quad 2HCl$$

The carbonyl chloride (phosgene) produced is extremely toxic and has been used as a poison gas in warfare. Tetrachloromethane was at one time used in portable fire extinguishers for electrical fires, but carbonyl chloride was produced when these were used. They are obsolete!

The resistance of tetrachloromethane to hydrolysis is due to the high activation energy for the reaction. Thermodynamically, the hydrolysis is favourable; using enthalpies of formation ΔH_f, we can find ΔH for the reaction

$$CCl_4 \quad + \quad 2H_2O \quad \rightarrow \quad CO_2 \quad + \quad 4HCl$$

$$\Delta H \quad = \quad \Delta H_f^{\ominus}(CO_2) \quad + \quad 4\Delta H_f^{\ominus}(HCl) - \Delta H_f^{\ominus}(CCl_4) - 2\Delta H_f^{\ominus}(H_2O)$$

$$= \quad (-393.5) \quad + \quad 4(-92.3) \quad - \quad (-129.6) \quad - \quad 2(-285.8)$$

$$= \quad -61.5 \text{ kJ mol}^{-1}$$

The mixture of tetrachloromethane and water is thermodynamically unstable. However, tetrachloromethane has no accessible orbitals which could accept electron pairs from water since all are used in bonding. In order for the reaction to occur, C–Cl bonds must be broken or at least weakened, and this results in a large activation energy for the process. The mixture is therefore kinetically stable.

This kinetic stability is a highly significant feature of carbon chemistry generally. Most carbon compounds are thermodynamically unstable with respect to oxidation or to hydrolysis – yet life needs oxygen and water. Fortunately the compounds are kinetically stable. Most reactions in inorganic chemistry operate under thermodynamic, not kinetic, control.

Silicon tetrachloride, $SiCl_4$, is rapidly attacked by water at room temperature:

$$SiCl_4(l) \quad + \quad 2H_2O(l) \quad \rightarrow \quad SiO_2(s) \quad + \quad 4HCl(aq)$$

The initial product is hydrated silica, $Si(OH)_4$, but this loses water quickly. The rapidity of the hydrolysis is due to the electron-pair donation by water into empty d-orbitals of the silicon atom. In this hydrolysis Si–Cl bonds (weaker in any case than C–Cl) do not have to be broken before Si–O bonds start to form. The activation energy for this hydrolysis is therefore much lower than for that of tetrachloromethane. It is not as low as that for boron trichloride, where a low-energy orbital is able to receive the lone-pair, so the hydrolysis of silicon tetrachloride is slower than that of boron trichloride.

Explain the difference between **thermodynamic** and **kinetic** stability.

Oxides of groups 3 and 4

Table 6.1 gives a summary of the main properties of these oxides. As expected the trend from non-metal to metal in both groups is shown by increasing basicity and ionic character in the oxides.

Table 6.1 *Some properties of the oxides of Groups 3 and 4*

Oxide	Nature	Example reactions
Group 3: B_2O_3	Acidic	Reacts readily with water: $B_2O_3 + 6H_2O \rightarrow 2 B(OH)_3$ $B(OH)_3$ is a monoprotic acid, ionising in water thus: $B(OH)_3 + 2H_2O \rightarrow B(OH)_4^- + H_3O^+$
Al_2O_3	Amphoteric	Freshly prepared Al_2O_3 reacts with HCl or NaOH: basic nature: $Al_2O_3 + 6HCl \rightarrow 2AlCl_3 + 3H_2O$ acidic nature: $Al_2O_3 + 3H_2O + 6NaOH \rightarrow 2Na_3Al(OH)_6$ (sodium aluminate)
Group 4: CO	Neutral	Does not react with water. With hot NaOH solution under pressure CO gives sodium methanoate: $CO + NaOH \rightarrow HCOONa$.
CO_2	Acidic	Dissolves in water to give the weak acid carbonic acid, H_2CO_3. $H_2CO_3 + H_2O \rightleftharpoons H_3O^+ + HCO_3^-$; $HCO_3^- + H_2O \rightleftharpoons CO_3^{2-} + H_3O^+$
SiO_2	Acidic	$SiO_2 + CaO \rightarrow CaSiO_3$ in blast furnace. NaOH needs to be molten or in hot concentrated aqueous solution: $SiO_2 + 2NaOH \rightarrow Na_2SiO_3 + H_2O$
PbO	Amphoteric	Basic nature: $PbO + 2HCl \rightarrow PbCl_2 + H_2O$. $PbCl_2$ dissolves in conc HCl to give soluble ions such as $PbCl_3^-$ and $PbCl_4^{2-}$. Acidic nature: $PbO + 2NaOH + 3H_2O \rightarrow Na_2Pb(OH)_6$, sodium plumbate(II).
PbO_2	Amphoteric	Basic nature: with ice-cold conc HCl, $PbCl_4$ is formed. If this is allowed to warm up it decomposes to chlorine and $PbCl_2$: this shows the (much more important) oxidising nature of lead(IV) oxide: $PbO_2 + 4HCl \rightarrow PbCl_4 + 2H_2O$; $PbCl_4 \rightarrow PbCl_2 + Cl_2$. Most other acids do not affect PbO_2. Acidic nature: with molten NaOH: $PbO_2 + 2NaOH \rightarrow Na_2PbO_3$(sodium Plumbate(IV)) + H_2O.
Pb_3O_4	Behaves as $2PbO.PbO_2$	$Pb_3O_4 + 4HNO_3 \rightarrow 2Pb(NO_3)_2 + PbO + 2H_2O$ This shows the greater acidity of PbO_2 compared with PbO. Lead(IV) oxide is not basic enough to react with dilute nitric acid.

The oxides of Group 3

Boron oxide B_2O_3 is strikingly different from any other oxide considered here. The sum of boron's first three ionisation energies is 6828 kJ mol^{-1}, too high to be compensated by ionic lattice enthalpy; and the B–O bond has a dissociation energy of 523 kJ mol^{-1} making it one of the strongest covalent bonds known. There is no B=O double bond. The result is that boron oxide shows complex polymeric arrangements, unlike the regular covalent structure of silicon dioxide. Boron oxide is acidic, reacting with water to give boric acid:

$$B_2O_3(s)   +   3H_2O \text{ (l)}   \rightarrow   2 B(OH)_3 \text{ (aq)}.$$

Boric acid is sometimes written H_3BO_3. It would appear to be tribasic (or triprotic), that is have three replaceable hydrogen ions per molecule, but the way it ionises makes it monobasic. Instead of donating H^+ ions, it accepts OH^- ions into its empty orbital, leaving H^+ free in the solvent:

$$B(OH)_3(aq) \; + \; 2H_2O(l) \; \rightarrow \; B(OH)_4^-(aq) \; + \; H_3O^+(aq)$$

Boron oxide shows no basic properties at all.

Aluminium oxide (alumina) is amphoteric, which classifies aluminium as a semi-metal on chemical grounds. A semi-metal has characteristics of both metal and non-metal. Judged on physical properties, aluminium is a metal. The amphoteric properties of aluminium oxide are difficult to show unless it is freshly made. Ageing even for a few hours gives a highly resistant crystal structure, corundum, which is unaffected by aqueous acid or base. Fresh alumina reacts thus:

as a base: $\qquad Al_2O_3(s) \; + \; 6HCl(aq) \rightarrow 2AlCl_3(aq) \; + \; 3H_2O(l)$

as an acid: $\qquad Al_2O_3(s) \; + \; 3H_2O(l) \; + \; 6NaOH(aq) \rightarrow 2Na_3Al(OH)_6(aq).$
$$\text{sodium aluminate}$$

You will see other ways of representing sodium aluminate, for example $NaAlO_2$. The composition of solid sodium aluminate depends on how the solution from which it comes has been treated, for example the amount of heating involved.

Aluminium hydroxide reacts readily with acid and base; addition of aqueous sodium hydroxide to a solution of aluminium ions gives a white gelatinous precipitate of aluminium hydroxide. This disappears with addition of excess alkali; if acid is added to the solution, the white precipitate of aluminium hydroxide returns, then with more acid gives a solution of the aluminium salt once more:

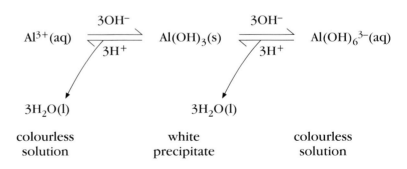

Figure 6.4 *The reaction of aluminium hydroxide with acid and alkali*

The oxides of Group 4
The acid/base character of the oxides of Group 4 was covered in Module 1, Chapter 5. The principal features of their chemistries are given in Table 6.1. (page 65).

Oxidation states in Group 4

The trend from oxidation state $+4$ in carbon to $+2$ in lead has been mentioned in Module 1 Chapter 5. Here the reasons for this behaviour are considered.

Carbon shows a range of oxidation states; $+4$ in CO_2, $+2$ in CO and -4 in CH_4. Tin and lead show $+4$ and $+2$, and $+2$ becomes more stable as the group is descended, in practice the difference being marked between tin and lead. Thus tin ($+2$) is reducing and finds a use in the production of phenylamine from nitrobenzene:

$$\text{(NO}_2\text{ benzene)} + 3Sn^{2+} + 7H^+ \rightarrow \text{(NH}_3^+\text{ benzene)} + 2H_2O + 3Sn^{4+}$$

Figure 6.5 Production of phenylamine from nitrobenzene

A mixture of tin and concentrated hydrochloric acid is used, which react when heated under reflux to give tin(II) chloride which is the reducing agent. Lead ($+2$) shows no such reducing properties.

Both tin (II) oxide, SnO, and tin(IV) oxide SnO_2, are amphoteric oxides, and react with hydrochloric acid in acid-base reactions to give the corresponding chloride;

$$SnO(s) + 2HCl(aq) \rightarrow SnCl_2(aq) + H_2O(l)$$

$$SnO_2(s) + 4HCl(aq) \rightarrow SnCl_4(aq) + 2H_2O(l)$$

Tin (IV) chloride is covalent, so the solution has to be kept acidic if the following hydrolysis is to be avoided:

$$SnCl_4(aq) +H_2O(l) \rightleftharpoons SnCl_3OH(aq) + HCl(aq)$$

With sodium hydroxide these oxides give soluble salts, sodium stannate(II) and sodium stannate(IV). They are not important.

Lead(IV) oxide is amphoteric. However, it is resistant to attack by most acids other than concentrated hydrochloric acid, and reacts only with molten, rather than aqueous, sodium hydroxide. The acid-base properties of lead(IV) oxide are unimportant. Much more significant is its oxidising power.

Tin(IV) oxide does not oxidise the chloride ion; with lead(IV) oxide PbO_2 the situation is wholly different. The $+4$ state of lead is strongly oxidising, and at room temperature concentrated HCl is oxidised to chlorine, lead ($+4$) being reduced to lead ($+2$.)

$$PbO_2(s) + 4HCl(aq) \rightarrow PbCl_2(s) + Cl_2(g) + 2H_2O(l).$$

Lead ($+2$) shows no reducing properties.

A scarlet oxide of lead, **A**, which contains the metal in two different oxidation states, reacts with aqueous nitric acid to give a solution of compound **B**, and a brown residue **C**. With sodium hydroxide solution **B** gives a white precipitate **D** which with further addition of sodium hydroxide gives a colourless solution **E**.
Residue **C** reacts with concentrated hydrochloric acid to give a pale yellow solution **F** and a green gas **G**, which will oxidise iodide ions to iodine. If **F** is diluted with water, a white solid **H** is precipitated.
Identify all the substances **A** to **H**, and give equations to represent all the reactions that are occurring.

The reason for these differences is related to the sizes of the atoms. The electron structure of group 4 atoms is $ns^2 np^2$. The atom could form an ion by loss of the p-electrons, or two covalent bonds by sharing, again using the p-orbitals. Both would give compounds with the group 4 atom in the +2 oxidation state. The (+4) state could be achieved by loss of all four electrons to give a 4+ ion, but even in the case of lead such an ion would be small enough to be very polarising, and the resultant compounds would be covalent. Alternatively, if one of the s electrons is promoted to the p, with one electron in each orbital, such an excited state can form four covalent bonds:

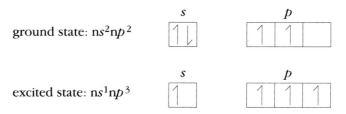

ground state: $ns^2 np^2$

excited state: $ns^1 np^3$

Figure 6.6 Formation of covalent bonds by electron promotion

The electron promotion is endothermic. It will occur if the energy required can be repaid by formation of the extra bonds, that is if the E–X bond strength is about a quarter of the promotional energy or more. This in turn will depend on the bond length: table 6.2 gives some values for bonds with chlorine. The bond strengths have been calculated from Born-Haber cycles.

Table 6.2 *Bond length and bond strength between Group 4 elements and chlorine.*

Bond	Bond length/pm	Bond strength/kJ mol^{-1}
C–Cl	177	346
Si–Cl	222	407
Sn–Cl	220	324
Pb–Cl	253	252

In the case of tin, the bonds formed are strong enough to compensate for the promotional energy of the s-electron, so tin(IV) chloride is more thermodynamically favoured than tin(II) chloride. With lead, the longer, weaker Pb–Cl bonds do not compensate energetically, and so ionic $PbCl_2$ with a lattice enthalpy of -2269 kJ mol^{-1} is thermodynamically more stable than covalent $PbCl_4$.

Similar arguments can be made for the oxides.

The extraction of aluminium

The purification of bauxite to give aluminium oxide

Aluminium is the commonest metal, being 8.1% of the Earth's crust by mass, and the third commonest element after oxygen (46.6%) and silicon (27.7%). This is because many rocks are aluminosilicates.

The ore of aluminium is bauxite, which is aluminium oxide with iron oxides and silicon dioxide as unwanted companions. Their proportion is quite high, so they cannot really be regarded as impurities.

Silicon dioxide is acidic, iron oxide basic, and aluminium oxide amphoteric. The separation process depends on these differences. The finely crushed ore is agitated with hot 10% aqueous sodium hydroxide solution, which will dissolve the amphoteric alumina but leaves the iron oxides and silicon dioxide which are filtered off. Although it is an acidic oxide, silicon dioxide needs a more concentrated alkali solution to dissolve it. This is a kinetic feature associated with its giant covalent structure.

The reaction of aluminium oxide with sodium hydroxide solution is:

$$Al_2O_3(s) \ + \ 6NaOH(aq) \ + \ 3H_2O(l) \ \rightarrow \ 2Na_3Al(OH)_6(aq)$$

The solution of sodium aluminate is filtered from the unwanted residues. Carbon dioxide is blown through the solution, which precipitates aluminium hydroxide since carbon dioxide is more acidic than alumina and so forms sodium bicarbonate:

$$Na_3Al(OH)_6(aq) \ + \ 3CO_2(aq) \ \rightarrow \ Al(OH)_3(s) \ + \ 3NaHCO_3(aq)$$

The aluminium hydroxide is filtered off and heated to form pure aluminium oxide:

$$2Al(OH)_3(s) \ \xrightarrow{\text{heat}} \ Al_2O_3(s) \ + \ 3H_2O(g)$$

All of these processes occur at the bauxite mine so that large quantities of unwanted waste, called gangue, are not transported large distances.

The extraction of aluminium from alumina

Aluminium is a reactive metal:

$$Al^{3+} \ + \ 3e^- \ \rightleftharpoons \ Al \qquad E^\ominus \ = \ -1.66V$$

Aluminium oxide cannot be reduced by carbon or carbon monoxide below 3000°C. This is not an achievable temperature on a large scale for a long time, so electrolysis is used. Aluminium was first produced commercially by H.S–C. Deville by reduction of aluminium chloride with sodium, a large scale plant being financially backed by Napoleon III and the metal being displayed at the Paris Exhibition in 1855. Napoleon's banquets for a time had the benefit of aluminium plate rather than silver or gold! In 1886 C.M. Hall in the USA and P.L.T Héroult in France discovered independently but virtually simultaneously that aluminium oxide will dissolve in molten cryolite, Na_3AlF_6, to give an electrolyte. The priority of one or the other was the cause of some acrimony

There is no particular answer to this; consider the ethical implications of purifying bauxite at the mine rather than in the UK.

Write equations to represent the reactions between

(a) aluminium chloride and sodium
(b) titanium(IV) chloride and sodium.

and resulted in a number of lawyers becoming considerably richer; now the contribution of each is acknowledged in the name of the Hall–Héroult Cell, (Figure 6.7.)

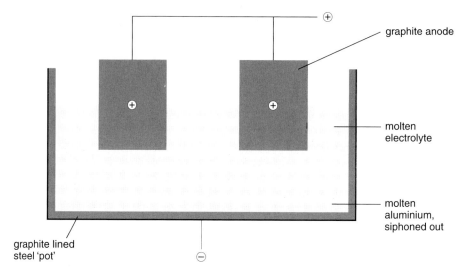

graphite anode

molten electrolyte

molten aluminium, siphoned out

graphite lined steel 'pot'

Figure 6.7 The Hall–Héroult cell.

Aluminium oxide melts at 2072 °C. This is not a feasible temperature for an electrolytic cell; Hall and Héroult's electrolyte of 90% molten Na_3AlF_6, (now synthetic, though originally mined in Greenland), 5% calcium fluoride and 5% alumina has a melting temperature around 900 °C. This is well above the melting temperature of 660 °C for aluminium.

Figure 6.8 The cell room at an aluminium smelter, using the Hall-Héroult cell method

Anodes are of carbon, made from petroleum coke, and the cathode is a graphite lining in a steel 'pot'. Each pot is about 5 × 10 × 1m deep, and will produce a tonne of aluminium per day. Ten anodes are suspended from a beam which can be raised or lowered hydraulically to keep the interelectrode spacing constant. This keeps the cell resistance – and therefore its temperature – constant also. As electrolysis proceeds, fresh alumina is added to the electrolyte and molten aluminium accumulates on the bottom of the cell. The space between this and the anodes is about 5mm. On average one anode per cell per day will need replacing, since the liberated oxygen reacts with it. The electrode reactions are complex, but can be represented:

cathode: $\qquad\qquad\qquad Al^{3+} + 3e^- \rightarrow Al$

anode: $\qquad 2O^{2-} + C \rightarrow CO_2 + 4e^-$

The carbon dioxide liberated has to be treated to remove dusts from the electrolyte which would be both wasteful and polluting. Aluminium smelters use a lot of energy, and are usually built near to plentiful energy sources, for example hydro-electric facilities or coal mines.

Molten aluminium is siphoned out of the cell periodically and alloyed to customer requirements before casting into rod or ingot according to its use for extrusion or for rolling into sheet.

Although Aluminium is expensive to produce, compared with iron which is about one-tenth the cost – but the metal is very important. It finds use in lightweight alloys (usually with magnesium) for aircraft and shipbuilding, and increasingly for use in motor vehicles. Improvements in fuel consumption will come from reduced weight of cars, since the aerodynamics are more or less optimum. Aluminium is easy to extrude into complex shapes, and can readily be cast and machined. Although reactive, it is a useful engineering metal because of the tough layer of oxide which is always present and which protects the metal from attack.

Carbon and its oxides in the iron and steel industry

Carbon is closely connected with the extraction and use of iron and steel; it, and carbon monoxide, are used to reduce iron ore in the blast furnace, and the proportion of carbon in the product determines whether the material is iron or steel.

The production of iron

Iron ore is usually iron(III) oxide, Fe_2O_3, which is basic. The impurities are mainly of silica, SiO_2, which is acidic. The blast furnace has been used since ancient times in one form or another to produce iron, but the modern form enables a continuous process of high efficiency.

The reactions in the furnace must do three things:

* reduce iron oxide Fe_2O_3 to iron, Fe

* remove the impurity material

* produce the necessary heat.

The 'inputs' needed to achieve this are

* iron ore

* coke   } from the top of the furnace

* limestone

* oxygen-enriched air blast at the base of the furnace.

The 'outputs' are

* iron containing about 4% carbon: 'pig' iron

* slag, mainly calcium silicate

* hot gases, mostly nitrogen but also containing CO_2 and CO.

The reactions in the furnace are complex and not fully understood. This may seem odd for such an old-established process, but the technology can be perfected even if the science is not fully appreciated. Metals have been smelted for millenia without a scientific understanding of the processes.

Figure 6.9 A blast furnace

The reactions, together with their effects, can be represented:

1 $C(s) + O_2(g) \rightarrow CO_2(g)$

around the blast inlet: produces heat.

2 $CO_2(g) + C(s) \rightarrow 2CO(g)$

further from the blast inlet; produces the reducing agent.

3 $Fe_2O_3(s) + 3CO(g) \rightarrow 2Fe(l) + 3CO_2(g)$

reduces the iron ore

4 $Fe_2O_3(s) + 3C(s) \rightarrow 2Fe(l) + 3CO(g)$

also a reducing reaction

5 $CaCO_3(s) \rightarrow CaO(s) + CO_2(g)$

produces basic CaO.

6 $CaO(s) + SiO_2(s) \rightarrow CaSiO_3(l)$

acid–base reaction; removes SiO_2 impurity as a molten slag and enables a continuous process.

Reactions 1, 3 and 6 are exothermic, the rest endothermic. Although addition of calcium carbonate as limestone enables impure ore to be used, the level of impurity is important since the formation of slag uses fuel and therefore is a significant cost.

Iron was originally smelted using charcoal; much of the mediaeval deforestation of England was due to charcoal production. In 1777 Abraham Darby showed that coke was a suitable substitute (coal is not), and this has been used ever since.

Molten iron collects at the bottom of the furnace, overlaid with molten slag. This is both less dense than and immiscible with the iron. The iron is tapped into large 'torpedoes', cylindrical containers which carry the molten iron on to the steel making process. Alternatively the iron can be used directly to make cast iron objects such as manhole and drain covers.

Cast or 'pig' iron contains about 4% carbon; it is hard, but very brittle, so if struck sharply it will break. The particular sort of toughness which it shows is ideal, however, in its chosen applications.

Steel is an alloy of carbon and iron containing between 0.5% and 2% of carbon. Mild steel has about 0.5% carbon. The molten pig iron is put in a furnace with a quantity of scrap steel, and magnesium powder blown in. This removes sulphur as magnesium sulphide slag which is skimmed off. Oxygen is then blown in and the carbon oxidises to carbon dioxide. When sufficient carbon has been removed, the molten steel can be cast and then rolled to whatever shape the customer requires, or alloyed as necessary. Various special steels are of considerable significance – see Table 6.3.

Table 6.3 *Some alloy steels.*

Steel	Alloying elements	Uses	Properties
Stainless	12–20% Cr, 8–10% Ni	surgical instruments, catering equipment	corrosion resistance
Vanadium	Vanadium	spanners	springy and tough
Tool	Tungsten	cutting tools	hard
Molybdenum	Molybdenum	various	increases malleability

The halogens

The elements

The word 'halogen' means salt-former, used because of the large number of ionic, salt-like compounds which Group 7 elements form. Chlorine is one of the most significant of industrial chemicals, produced on an enormous scale.

Figure 7.1 Iodine

Figure 7.2 Bromine

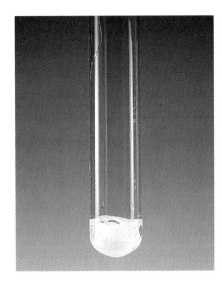

Figure 7.3 Chlorine

The physical properties of the elements

The principal physical properties of the halogens are given in table 7.1.

Table 7.1 *Principal physical properties of the halogens*

Element	State at room temperature	Melting temperature/°C	Boiling temperature/°C	Atomic radius/pm	Ionic radius/pm
fluorine	pale yellow gas	−220	−188	72	136
chlorine	greenish gas	−101	−34.7	99	181
bromine	brown volatile liquid	−7.2	58.8	114	195
iodine	dark grey lustrous solid	114	184	133	216

The forces between the diatomic molecules X_2 of the halogens are van der Waals' forces, so the melting and boiling temperatures increase with increasing size of the molecules. The atomic radius increases with increasing atomic mass and hence increasing number of shells; in every case the size of the anion is greater than that of the parent atom since repulsions increase with the addition of the extra electron.

Table 7.2 *Some further properties of the halogens*

Element	1st ionisation energy/ kJ mol^{-1}	Electron affinity kJ mol^{-1}	Standard reduction potential/ V	Bond dissociation enthalpy/ kJ mol^{-1}
fluorine	1680	−348	+2.87	158
chlorine	1260	−364	+1.36	242
bromine	1140	−342	+1.07	193
iodine	1010	−314	+0.54	151

Draw (small) graphs of the properties in table 7.1 vs atomic number.

Draw (small) graphs of the properties in table 7.2 vs atomic number.

The ionisation energies (Table 7.2) show the expected trend with increasing size of the atom, and are the second highest of all atoms within the same period since the atoms are the second smallest; in both respects they are exceeded only by the inert gases. Knowledge of the ionisation energies is less useful than for metals. Halogens in positive oxidation states do not form positive ions as such, but are bonded covalently to more electronegative atoms, as in the oxyanions OCl^- and ClO_3^-, for example.

The electron affinities show a peak at chlorine. Since fluorine is the smallest atom with the fewest electrons, it might be thought that it would attract electrons most strongly of all. The electron is being added to an atom of small volume, however, and the repulsions from other electrons are therefore disproportionately large. The remaining electron affinities fall with increasing size of the atom, as might be expected with the accompanying fall in effective nuclear charge.

The standard reduction potentials follow the expected trend; the smaller the atom, the more likely it is to be reduced. The large value for fluorine reflects in part the very large hydration enthalpy of the fluoride ion, −506 kJ mol^{-1}, against −364 kJ mol^{-1} for chloride.

The bond dissociation enthalpies show a peak at chlorine; the usual rule is that the shorter a bond is, the stronger it is, but it is possible to have too much of a good thing and in the case of fluorine the non-bonding electrons are brought so close together that they repel, and weaken the bond compared with what might have been expected. This feature is part of the reason for fluorine's very reactive nature, the high lattice enthalpies or bond enthalpies in the compounds produced being the other part of the picture.

Tests for the halogens

There are various tests which can be used to identify chlorine, bromine and iodine, but there is no test common to all three.

Chlorine

The tests for chlorine employ its strongly oxidising character.

Moist litmus paper is bleached rapidly; the colour is a pigment from a lichen, and chlorine oxidises it to colourless products. If blue litmus is used, it very briefly turns red before being bleached.

Chlorine
Bleaches litmus paper but slowly
Oxidises Br^- to Br_2
Oxidises I^- to I_2
Turns starch-iodide paper blue-black

Chlorine will oxidise bromides to bromine, and iodides to iodine. In both cases the solutions turn brown, though that of iodine is much darker and if excess chlorine is used solid iodine will precipitate. The first of these reactions

$$Cl_2(aq) \quad + \quad 2Br^-(aq) \quad \rightarrow \quad Br_2(aq) \quad + \quad 2Cl^-(aq)$$

is used to obtain bromine from seawater, so isn't just of analytical interest. If an immiscible organic solvent is added to the reaction mixtures, for example hexane, the organic layer will be coloured brown with bromine, or purple with iodine.

Moist starch-iodide paper (paper impregnated with starch and potassium iodide) turns blue-black with chlorine. The iodide ions in the paper are oxidised to iodine, and the starch then reacts with this to give a blue-black compound.

Bromine

Bromine will bleach litmus paper, but does so much more slowly than chlorine.

Bromine liberates iodine from iodides in aqueous solution; the solution darkens, and an immiscible organic solvent can be used to show the presence of iodine, turning purple.

Bromine turns moist starch–iodide paper blue black, for the same reasons as chlorine does.

Bromine will react with paper moistened with the dye fluorescein to turn it scarlet. The product is eosin, an ingredient of red ink.

Bromine
Bleaches litmus paper but slowly
Liberates iodine from iodide solutions
Turns starch–iodine paper blue-black
Turns fluorescein scarlet

Iodine

Iodine is without effect on litmus.

Iodine will turn moist starch–iodide paper blue-black, but will also do the same to starch solution alone, which neither chlorine nor bromine will do.

Iodine is purple in solution in organic solvents which have no oxygen, for example hexane or methylbenzene. The presence of oxygen in a solvent give a browner cast to the solution, so the antiseptic Tincture of Iodine, which is a solution in ethanol, is brown. This difference in colour can be used as a qualitative test for oxygen-containing solvents in organic chemistry.

Iodine
No effect on litmus paper
Turns starch solution blue-black
Is purple in organic solvents without oxygen

The hydrogen halides

All the halogens form covalent hydrides H–X, which are colourless gases at room temperature and which give misty fumes in moist air. All but hydrogen fluoride can be made by direct combination of the elements, but mixtures of hydrogen gas and fluorine gas explode, even at low temperatures. Hydrogen chloride is made industrially by burning hydrogen in chlorine:

$$H_2(g) \quad + \quad Cl_2(g) \quad \rightarrow \quad 2HCl(g)$$

This is the major use for the hydrogen and chlorine coproducts from the Gibb's Diphragm cell for the production of sodium hydroxide (chapter 5, page 55). A mixture of the gases in the dark will not react; in diffused sunlight hydrogen chloride will be produced 'smoothly', a term used to indicate that the reaction did not spread itself and the chemist all over the countryside. Bright sunlight causes the mixture to explode. Hydrogen and bromine react similarly, though less violently. In both cases the reaction has a radical mechanism.

Hydrogen and iodine combine rather poorly; at 400°C with a platinum catalyst an equilibrium is set up so conversion to products is incomplete. This reaction was the basis of the classic early experiments on chemical equilibrium by Bodenstein, and is covered further in Module 2, Chapter 3.

None of these methods affords a practical laboratory preparation, so the action of sulphuric acid (for HF and HCl) or phosphoric acid H_3PO_4 (for HBr and HI) on the appropriate sodium halide is used instead. These points are dealt with further below (page 78).

All of the hydrogen halides are very water-soluble, giving very acidic solutions. It is important in equations to give the state of HCl, since the symbols for the gas and the aqueous solution would otherwise be the same.

The strength of the hydrohalic acids

The high solubility of the hydrogen halides in water is largely due to the high hydration enthalpy of the hydrogen ion and the relatively small halide ions, compensating for the bond dissociation enthalpy of the molecule. The dissocation

$$HX(aq) \quad + \quad H_2O(l) \quad \rightleftharpoons \quad H_3O^+(aq) \quad + \quad X^-(aq)$$

is responsible for the acidity. The extent to which a molecule H-A dissociates in solution depends on

- the strength of the H–X bond;

- the nature of the solvent and its interaction with the ions H^+ and X^- once they are formed;

- any factors which stabilise the ion X^- compared with the undissociated molecule HX.

Applying these criteria to the hydrohalic acids, the only one of significance is the strength of the hydrogen – halogen bond; the effect of anion stabilisation arises only with the oxyacids, and is referred to briefly later. Thus the decreasing bond strength from H–Cl to H–I (Table 7.3) arising from the increase in size of the halogen atom makes HI(aq) the strongest of these three acids. The differences in water are not practically evident, however, and HI(aq) behaves essentially as HCl(aq) in terms of acidity. Hydriodic acid is actually seldom met with; it has no acidic properties that are more useful than hydrochloric acid, and it is easily oxidised to iodine by atmospheric oxygen and therefore does not keep very well.

Table 7.3 *Some further properties of the halogens*

bond	H–F	H–Cl	H–Br	H–I
bond enthalpy/ kJ mol^{-1}	562	431	366	299

Hydrofluoric acid is the odd one out. Aqueous HF behaves as a weak acid, but there is argument as to whether HF(aq) really is weak or whether it simply appears to be so because of other properties not directly related to its acidity. In Chapter 3 of module 1 the considerable hydrogen bonding in liquid HF was explored, and the effect of this on its boiling temperature noted. The H–F bond is indeed the strongest of the four, but this factor alone is probably not enough to explain the difference in acid strength. The ability of fluoride ions to form hydrogen bonds with undissociated HF molecules is also a factor:

$$H\text{–}F(aq) \quad + \quad F^-(aq) \quad \rightarrow \quad [F\text{-}\text{-}\text{-}\text{-}H\text{-}F]^-(aq)$$

This reaction effectively prevents HF molecules from dissociating. Salts such as KHF_2 can be prepared.

Hydrogen fluoride dissolves glass, and for this reason is popularly thought to be the most corrosive of acids. It gives extremely unpleasant and painful burns which take a long time to heal, but is not especially corrosive otherwise. Its ability to attack glass comes from the formation of the ion SiF_6^{2-}, which is water-soluble; other halide ions are too large to fit around the silicon atom, and so do not form similar complexes. Solutions of HF are kept in poly(ethene) bottles.

Some aspects of the chemistry of halide salts

The tests for halide ions

The usual test for halide ions other than fluoride uses the insolubility of silver halides. The test solution is made acidic with dilute nitric acid to ensure the removal of carbonate or sulphite ions which would interfere by giving a spurious precipitate, and then aqueous silver nitrate solution is added. A white precipitate indicates chloride, a pale creamy precipitate bromide, and a yellow precipitate iodide. The general equation representing the reaction is

$$X^-(aq) \quad + \quad Ag^+(aq) \quad \rightleftharpoons \quad AgX(s)$$

The precipitates can further be distinguished by their reaction with ammonia solution. The effect of ammonia in this test depends on the equilibrium where ammonia complexes with aqueous silver ions to form diamminesilver(I) :

$$Ag^+(aq) \quad + \quad 2NH_3(aq) \quad \rightleftharpoons \quad [Ag(NH_3)_2]^+(aq).$$

This reaction reduces the concentration of silver ions in the solution. All these silver halides are sparingly soluble; the solubilities are given in table 7.4.

Table 7.4 *The solubilities of silver halides in mol dm^{-3} at 25°C.*

Halide	AgCl	AgBr	AgI
Solubility/mol dm^{-3}	1.34×10^{-5}	8.80×10^{-7}	9.10×10^{-9}

Silver chloride is sufficently soluble to enable the equilibrium given above to remove enough silver ions from the solution using dilute ammonia so that the solubility of silver chloride is not exceeded. Silver bromide is less soluble and so concentrated ammonia is required to move the equilibrium sufficiently to the right to have the same effect. Silver iodide is too insoluble, so the equilibrium cannot remove sufficient silver ions in this case and the precipitate does not dissolve.

These results are summarised in the test box. The test cannot be used for fluorides since silver fluoride is water-soluble.

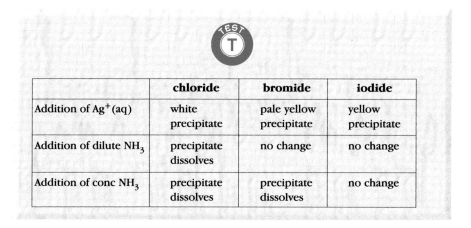

	chloride	bromide	iodide
Addition of Ag⁺(aq)	white precipitate	pale yellow precipitate	yellow precipitate
Addition of dilute NH₃	precipitate dissolves	no change	no change
Addition of conc NH₃	precipitate dissolves	precipitate dissolves	no change

An alternative method of testing for bromide and iodide ions is to oxidise them to the respective halogen, then shake with an immiscible organic solvent such as hexane. If the test solution is made acidic with nitric acid, a little hexane added followed by a little sodium chlorate(I) solution, shaking will produce a brown organic layer if bromide ions are present, and a purple one if iodide ions are present.

The reactions of halide salts with concentrated sulphuric acid

The halides react with concentrated sulphuric acid in the manner determined by the ease of oxidation of the halide ion. Thus sodium chloride does not give chlorine since sulphuric acid will not oxidise chloride ions; bromides and iodides do, however, give the halogen.

Sodium chloride reacts with concentrated sulphuric acid at any temperature obtainable in glass apparatus to give hydrogen chloride as misty fumes, and sodium hydrogen sulphate:

$$NaCl(s) \ + \ H_2SO_4(l) \ \rightarrow \ HCl(g) \ + \ NaHSO_4(s)$$

In a closed vessel this reaction is an equilibrium, arising because sulphuric acid is a stronger acid than hydrochloric acid; the relatively weak base Cl⁻ will therefore accept a proton. In an open system the hydrogen chloride gas escapes, so the equilibrium is not established. This process was at one time used for the industrial production of hydrochloric acid.

Both bromide ions and iodide ions are stronger reducing agents than chloride ions; being larger, their electrons are removed more readily. Bromide ions reduce sulphuric acid to sulphur dioxide. The products from the reaction are a mixture of hydrogen bromide and bromine:

$$NaBr(s) \ + \ H_2SO_4(l) \ \rightarrow \ HBr(g) \ + \ NaHSO_4(s)$$

$$2HBr(g) \ + \ H_2SO_4(l) \ \rightarrow \ Br_2(l) \ + \ 2H_2O(l) \ + \ SO_2(g)$$

The state symbols should be cautiously interpreted; the reaction mixture is a mess, and some sulphur dioxide will remain in solution as sulphurous acid, some of the bromine will be lost as a gas.

Iodide ions are bigger than bromide ions and are even more reducing; they will reduce sulphuric acid in three ways, all of which occur if sodium iodide is added to concentrated sulphuric acid at room temperature. No usable amounts of HI are produced, and the mixture is even more of a mess, being sludgily brown with purple iodine vapour being evolved, together with the delicate overtones of bad eggs from hydrogen sulphide. The four reactions are:

$$NaI(s) \ + \ H_2SO_4(l) \ \rightarrow \ HI(g) \ + \ NaHSO_4(s)$$

$$8HI(g) \ + \ H_2SO_4(l) \ \rightarrow \ 4I_2(s) \ + \ H_2S(g) \ + \ 4H_2O(l)$$

$$6HI(g) \ + \ H_2SO_4(l) \ \rightarrow \ 3I_2(s) \ + \ S(s) \ + \ 3H_2O(l)$$

$$2HI(g) \ + \ H_2SO_4(l) \ \rightarrow \ I_2(s) \ + \ SO_2(g) \ + \ 2H_2O(l)$$

The brown colour is due to the production of the tri-iodide ion from iodine and excess iodide:

$$I_2 \ + \ I^- \ \rightleftharpoons \ I_3^-$$

Explain in terms of atomic properties why the reducing ability of halide ions changes $Cl^- < Br^- < I^-$.

Draw a dot-and-cross diagram to show the bonding in the ion I_3^-, and state its shape, with reasons.

Positive oxidation states in the chemistry of chlorine

Chlorine is the third most electronegative element after fluorine and oxygen, so when in combination with these elements it shows positive oxidation states. The commonest compounds show chlorine $(+1)$ in sodium chlorate(I) or sodium hypochlorite $NaOCl$, and $(+5)$ in sodium chlorate(V), $NaClO_3$, often just called sodium chlorate.

Sodium chlorate(I) is common household bleach, which is made by electrolysis of aqueous sodium chloride (see also Chapter 5) at room temperature but allowing the chlorine and sodium hydroxide produced to mix:

$$2NaOH(aq) \ + \ Cl_2(aq) \rightarrow NaOCl(aq) \ + \ NaCl(aq) \ + \ H_2O(l)$$
$$\qquad\qquad\quad (0) \qquad\qquad (+1) \qquad\quad (-1)$$

Ionic equations are often preferable:

$$2OH^-(aq) + Cl_2(aq) \rightarrow OCl^-(aq) + Cl^-(aq) + H_2O(l)$$
$$\quad\quad\quad\quad (0) \quad\quad\quad (+1) \quad\quad (-1)$$

The oxidation states of the chlorine are shown; the element has been simultaneously oxidised and reduced, so has undergone disproportionation (see also Chapter 2). If the electrolysis is carried out at a higher temperature, around 80°C, then the reaction occurring is:

$$6NaOH(aq) + 3Cl_2(aq) \rightarrow NaClO_3(aq) + 5NaCl(aq) + 3H_2O(l)$$
$$\quad\quad\quad\quad\quad (0) \quad\quad\quad\quad (+5) \quad\quad\quad (-1)$$

The elemental chlorine has disproportionated in a different manner. The chlorate(I) ion will also disproportionate if heated in aqueous solution:

$$3\,OCl^-(aq) \rightarrow 2Cl^-(aq) + ClO_3^-(aq)$$
$$\quad (+1) \quad\quad\quad (-1) \quad\quad (+5)$$

The oxyacids themselves, HOCl and HClO$_3$, are seldom met; the oxyanions are oxidising agents in acidic solution, though, and are sometimes used as more convenient oxidising agents than the halogens themselves:

$$ClO^-(aq) + 2H^+(aq) + 2e^- \rightarrow Cl^-(aq) + H_2O(l)$$

$$ClO_3^-(aq) + 6H^+(aq) + 6e^- \rightarrow Cl^-(aq) + 3H_2O(l)$$

Commercial bleach is sodium chlorate(I), as already mentioned; for most purposes, it does not matter that the solution also contains a lot of sodium chloride, so manufacturers don't go to the expense of separating it. It does mean, though, that if acids are added to domestic bleach, chlorine is evolved:

$$OCl^-(aq) + 2H^+(aq) + Cl^-(aq) \rightarrow Cl_2(g) + H_2O(l)$$

This is why the labels on bottles of bleach tell you not to mix it with any other material, such as other domestic cleaning materials containing the acid salt NaHSO$_4$.

Oxidation reactions of the halogens

All of the halogens are strong oxidising agents, the oxidising power decreasing as the size of the halogen increases:

Give the equation representing the reaction of fluorine with water at room temperature.

	$E^\ominus$/V
$F_2(g) + 2e^- \rightleftharpoons 2F^-(aq)$	+ 2.87
$Cl_2(aq) + 2e^- \rightleftharpoons 2Cl^-(aq)$	+ 1.36
$Br_2(aq) + 2e^- \rightleftharpoons 2Br^-(aq)$	+ 1.09
$I_2(aq) + 2e^- \rightleftharpoons 2I^-(aq)$	+ 0.54

The considerable oxidising power of fluorine is evident; it has the most positive potential of all half-cells, and will react with water itself so is quoted slightly differently in the table above. The reasons for the aggressive behaviour of fluorine have already been mentioned, that is its low bond enthalpy, the high hydration enthalpy of the fluoride ion, and the high bond strength of covalent bonds with other atoms. The reactions of fluorine are often so different from those of the other halogens that fluorine chemistry is a considerable speciality in its own right, far beyond our present concerns.

The potentials for the other halogens mean that any halogen will oxidise the ions of those halogens below it in the group. Thus chlorine will oxidise bromide and iodide ions, and bromine will oxidise iodide ions. The principal use of this industrially is the extraction of bromine from seawater; about 30,000 tonnes are produced annually in the UK, mostly for the manufacture of 1,2-dibromoethane which is used as an additive for leaded petrol and as an intermediate in the production of ethane-1,2-diol for antifreeze and hydraulic fluid. The details of the bromine extraction are not important; the reaction is essentially

$$Cl_2(aq) \quad + \quad 2Br^-(aq) \quad \rightarrow \quad 2Cl^-(aq) \quad + \quad Br_2(aq)$$

Pesticides, polymers and refrigerants

Chlorine is used in the manufacture of pesticides and herbicides, poly(chloroethene) or polyvinyl chloride, PVC, and in chlorofluorocarbons or CFCs used as refrigerants.

If two lines could encapsulate what many people regard as chemistry's greatest environmental horrors, the last two would be strong candidates. All of these materials get a bad press, and that of course is where most people get their chemical information; the press, or at least the media generally. The arguments presented are usually simplistic, often inaccurate, and since everyone who writes (including me) has their own agenda, the information presented can often be misinformation or even disinformation.

Environmental concern is a wholly proper concern; consequently all manufacturing processes are subject to an environmental audit. This is an assessment of the benefits of a product, the manufacturing costs in terms of raw materials and the impact of their extraction, energy consumption, unwanted co-products, transport implications, disposal; a whole host of inter-related and complex questions. These are not answered by simplistic notions such as the call to ' ban the use of organochlorine compounds' which some pressure groups have made. Chlorine has saved millions of lives through the massive improvements in public health brought about by water and sewage treatment, refrigeration, and the elimination of malaria from large areas of the world. To believe that this should all be written off is more than just simple-minded. This is not the place to expand further; an excellent account of PVC and the environment, for example, is given in John Emsley's book *The Consumer's Good Chemicals Guide*, and this is recommended.

For the conversion of 1,2-dibromoethane to ethan-1,2-diol suggest

(a) a suitable method,
(b) a mechanism for the reaction.

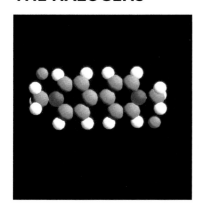

Figure 7.5 Chemical structure of paraquat (top) and its effects (above)

Pesticides and herbicides

DDT, dichlorodiphenyltrichloroethane, has been widely used as an insecticide. It has eliminated malaria from several areas of the world by killing the *Anopheles* mosquito which carries the malarial parasite, and has been used against many other insect pests. It has two problems, though; insects reproduce quite quickly, and so resistant strains are now found of many pests which formerly could be dealt with using DDT – and it breaks down very slowly in the environment.

Polychlorinated organic molecules, that is, ones containing more than one chlorine on a given carbon atom, hydrolyse much less readily than monochloro compounds such as chloroethane. DDT is almost insoluble in water, but has nevertheless found its way into food chains. The effects of this have been seen mainly in birds of prey, the eggs of which are rendered brittle by the presence of DDT in their food. Some populations of these animals have suffered badly as a result. DDT is still made and used, but on a much smaller scale than used to be the case, and the USA has banned domestic use completely though still makes it for export.

Herbicides are chemical weeders; principally developed to remove weeds from cereal crops, since the cereals are grasses and the herbicides affect only broad-leaved plants, they are manufactured under carefully controlled conditions. This is because the principal compounds, 2,4-D and 2,4,5-T, at one time contained too high a level of the extremely toxic compounds called dioxins. Very careful manufacturing is needed to prevent dioxin formation.

Figure 7.6 Pesticides and herbicides

PVC

Poly(chloroethene) is the systematic name for polyvinyl chloride, or PVC. The monomer, chloroethene or vinyl chloride is made from ethene (from cracking alkane fractions from crude oil) and chlorine, a useful coproduct being hydrogen chloride:

$$CH_2=CH_2 \ + \ Cl_2 \ \rightarrow \ CH_2\!-\!CH_2 \ \xrightarrow{heat} \ CH_2=CHCl \ + \ HCl$$

PVC finds extremely wide use in packaging, insulation, piping, guttering, in which there are no substitutes which have all the advantages of PVC. The manufacture of PVC is no more environmentally damaging than any other polymer. 1,2-Dichloroethane and vinyl chloride are both too reactive to survive to the upper atmosphere and cause ozone layer depletion, and the health hazards of vinyl chloride are well documented and the processes well controlled.

CFCs

Chlorofluorocarbons are nontoxic, inert compounds which have found wide use as aerosol propellants and as the cooling medium in refrigerators. They consist of various proportions of fluorine and chlorine attached to carbon, three examples being shown.

Figure 7.7 A use of PVC

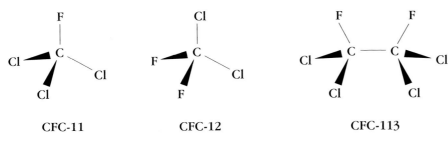

CFC-11 CFC-12 CFC-113

Figure 7.8 Some chlorofluorocarbon structures

Their use as aerosol propellants is being discontinued, since alternatives are available. Eventually their use in refrigerators will probably cease, but at the moment there are no suitable alternative materials although much work is in hand to find replacements.

The problem with CFCs lies in their stability unless they are irradiated with ultraviolet light. If they escape into the atmosphere, they do not hydrolyse or oxidise, but rise to the stratosphere. There, ultraviolet light causes their decomposition to, amongst other things, chlorine atoms. Also in the stratosphere, the conversion of oxygen to ozone occurs via the reaction

$$3O_2(g) \quad \rightarrow \quad 2O_3(g)$$

This ozone layer shields the Earth from a considerable amount of the incident ultraviolet radiation from the Sun. The problem is that the reverse reaction, where ozone decomposes to oxygen, is catalysed by chlorine atoms. CFCs have therefore been blamed for depletion of the ozone layer. They are not the only culprits by a long way; volcanic eruptions, for example, produce enormous quantities of ozone-depleting compounds.

Examination questions

1 (a) Using the following data, construct a Born-Haber cycle for potassium chloride and use it to find the electron affinity of chlorine.

	ΔH/kJ mol^{-1}
First ionisation energy of potassium	$+419$
Enthalpy of atomisation of potassium	$+89.2$
Enthalpy of atomisation of chlorine	$+121.7$
Enthalpy of formation of potassium chloride	-436.7
Lattice enthalpy of potassium chloride	-711

(6)

(b) Calcium is in the same period in the Periodic Table as potassium. The lattice enthalpy of calcium chloride is -2258 kJ mol^{-1}. Why is this so different from the value for potassium chloride given in (a)? **(2)**

(c) The thermal stability of group 2 carbonates increases from beryllium, the carbonate of which decomposes at room temperature, to barium, the carbonate of which is stable even at quite high temperatures. Explain this trend. **(4)**

(d) For the reaction

$$CaCO_3(s) \rightleftharpoons (CaO(s) + CO_2(g)$$

The equilibrium total pressure at 1200 K is 4 atm. Determine K_p. **(3)**

Total 15 marks

2 This question concerns redox behaviour, and the following data will be found useful.

	$E^{\ominus}$/V
$Fe^{3+}(aq) + e^- \rightleftharpoons Fe^{2+}(aq)$	$+0.77$
$\frac{1}{2}Cl_2(g) + e^- \rightleftharpoons Cl^-(aq)$	$+1.36$
$MnO_4^-(aq) + 8H^+(aq) + 5e^- \rightleftharpoons Mn^{2+}(aq) + 4H_2O(l)$	$+1.52$

(a) In potassium manganate(VII) titrations, the solutions are acidified with dilute sulphuric acid

(i) Using the data above, explain why dilute hydrochloric acid is not used for this purpose. **(3)**

(ii) Why is potassium manganate(VII) usually placed in the burette, despite the difficulties it presents in reading the burette? **(2)**

(b) A test for Mn^{2+} ions in solution is to react them with sodium bismuthate(V), $NaBiO_3$, in the presence of nitric acid. A purple colour will develop owing to the formation of MnO_4^- ions in the solution. The ionic half equation for the reduction of BiO_3^- ion is:

$$BiO_3^- + 6H^+ + 2e^- \rightleftharpoons Bi^{3+} + 3H_2O$$

(i) Use this half equation and the data above to write an ionic equation for the oxidation of the Mn^{2+} ion. **(2)**

(ii) Suggest, qualitatively, how the $E^{\ominus}$ value for $BiO_3^-|Bi^{3+}$ compares with that for $MnO_4^-|Mn^{2+}$. **(1)**

(c) An alloy contains iron and manganese only. On warming with dilute nitric acid 2.30g of this alloy gave a solution containing iron(III) ions and manganese(II) ions. Treatment of this solution with excess sodium bismuthate(V) completely oxidised all the Mn^{2+} ions present to MnO_4^- ions.

The excess bismuthate(V) ions were then completely destroyed and the solution made up to 250 cm^3 with distilled water and thoroughly shaken.

Titration of 25.0 cm^3 portions of this solution required 25.0 cm^3 of standard 0.100 mol dm^{-3} iron(II) sulphate solution.

(i) Write the equation for the reaction occurring during the titration. **(2)**

(ii) Calculate the percentage of manganese present in the alloy. **(5)**

Total 15 marks

3 (a) Write an expression for K_p for each of the following equilibria, giving the units in each case.

(i) $N_2O_4(g) \rightleftharpoons 2NO_2(g)$

(ii) $CaCO_3(s) \rightleftharpoons CaO(s) + CO_2(g)$ **(4)**

(b) How would the numerical value of K_p change if $BaCO_3$ were to be used in place of $CaCO_3$ in (a)(ii)? Explain your answer from your knowledge of the trends in the properties of the ions of Group 2 elements. **(3)**

(c) (i) With reference to the equilibrium in (a)(i), calculate the partial pressures of N_2O_4 and NO_2 at 60 °C and 1 atmosphere pressure, given that 81.3% of the initial N_2O_4 is dissociated at this temperature.

(ii) Calculate K_p at this temperature. **(5)**

(d) Use the mole fractions of NO_2 and N_2O_4 in the equilibrium mixture to calculate the apparent relative molecular mass at this temperature. **(2)**

Total 14 marks

4 (a) The following table shows some physical properties of two s-block metals.

Metal	Hardness	Melting temperature/ °C	Density/g cm^{-3}
caesium	very soft	28.7	1.9
barium	quite hard	714	3.51

(i) Suggest reasons for the differences in the physical properties of caesium and barium as shown in the table. The metals have the same crystal structure. **(3)**

(ii) Caesium gets its name from the blue colour it or its salts impart to a Bunsen flame. What process within the atom is responsible for the emission of this colour? **(1)**

(iii) If the light emitted from excited caesium atoms is passed through a spectrometer, what would you expect to see? **(1)**

(b) Sodium burns in excess oxygen to give a yellow solid, **Y**.

   (i) **Y** contains 58.97% sodium. Find its empirical formula. **(2)**

   (ii) The relative molecular mass of **Y** is 78. What is its molecular formula? **(1)**

   (iii) If **Y** is reacted with ice-cold dilute sulphuric acid, a solution of **Z** is obtained which will react with potassium manganate(VII) solution. Describe the experimental procedure you would use to determine the mole ratio in which **Z** and potassium manganate(VII) react together. **(3)**

Total 11 marks

5 (a) Sodium hydroxide is manufactured using the Gibbs Diaphragm Cell with an electrolyte of purified saturated brine.

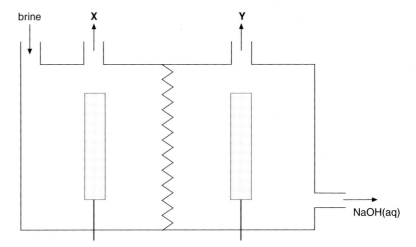

   (i) Label the anode and the cathode on the diagram. **(1)**

   (ii) Write equations for the reactions at the anode and cathode. **(2)**

   (iii) What is the main impurity in the sodium hydroxide product? **(1)**

   (iv) The main impurities in the brine which must be removed before electrolysis are magnesium and calcium ions. Suggest a reason why they must be removed **(2)**

(b) Electrolysis of brine under different conditions gives sodium chlorate(I); in this case the sodium hydroxide and chlorine are allowed to mix at room temperature.

   (i) Give the ionic equation for the reaction of chlorine with cold dilute aqueous sodium hydroxide. **(1)**

   (ii) If the solution of sodium chlorate(I) is heated, the chlorate(I) ion disproportionates. Write the ionic equation for the reaction, and use it to explain the meaning of disproportionation. **(3)**

(c) Give one use for

   (i) sodium hydroxide: **(1)**

   (ii) chlorine: **(1)**

   (iii) substance **Y** on the diagram **(1)**

(d) Suggest how using a solution of sodium chlorate(I), or otherwise, you could distinguish between separate aqueous solutions of potassium bromide and potassium iodide. **(4)**

Total 17 marks

6 (a) Sodium hydroxide is manufactured by an electrolytic process using a diaphragm cell.

(i) What is used as the electrolyte? **(1)**

(ii) Of what material is each of the anode and cathode made? **(2)**

(iii) Give an equation for the reaction occurring at each of the electrodes. **(2)**

(iv) Give one reason why it is necessary to have the two electrodes in separate compartments **(1)**

(v) Write an equation for the overall cell reaction. **(1)**

(b) Give one large-scale industrial use for each of the following:

(i) chlorine **(1)**

(ii) hydrogen **(1)**

(c) Iron(III) oxide is a basic oxide. What type of oxide is:

(i) aluminium oxide **(1)**

(ii) silicon dioxide **(1)**

(d) Bauxite is an ore containing hydrated aluminium oxide, iron(III) oxide and silicon dioxide. In order to obtain a purer form of aluminium oxide, bauxite is heated with a 10% solution of sodium hydroxide in which the aluminium oxide dissolves.

(i) Write an equation for the reaction of aluminium hydroxide with sodium hydroxide. **(2)**

(ii) Why does iron(III) oxide not dissolve in sodium hydroxide? **(1)**

(iii) Why does silicon dioxide not dissolve in a 10% solution of sodium hydroxide? **(1)**

Total 15 marks

7 (a) (i) How does concentrated sulphuric acid react with sodium chloride? Write an equation for the reaction. Suggest an appropriate temperature at which it might be carried out.

(ii) Sodium iodide does not react in this way. Give an equation for the reaction which occurs and explain the difference. **(4)**

(b) By reference to the structure and bonding in hydrogen fluoride explain why it is a much weaker acid than other halogen hydrides. **(3)**

(c) Given samples of chloride and iodide salts, how would you distinguish them other than by using concentrated sulphuric acid? **(3)**

(d) (i) On the basis of the redox potentials

$$E^{\ominus} / V$$

$Cl_2 + 2e^- \quad 2Cl^- \qquad +1.36$

$Br_2 + 2e^- \quad 2Br^- \qquad +1.09$

explain what occurs when chlorine is bubbled into a solution containing bromide ions.

(ii) What is the industrial significance of this reaction? **(5)**

Total 15 marks

Index

Use of *italics* indicates an illustration.